Heal
All and Everything

Healing
All and Everything

Leonard Locker

Element Books

Printed by Billings, Hylton Road,
Worcester
Designed by Humphrey Stone
Cover painting by Ken Evans from the collection
Thoughts in Solitude

Contents

Contents

Acknowledgements

I would like to express my sincere thanks to my many dowser friends who have directly or indirectly helped me in writing this book, and above all to that great dowser and healer, Bill Lewis, who set me on the healing path.

No man is an *Iland*, intire of it selfe; every man is a peece of the *Continent*, a part of the *maine;* if a *Clod* bee washed away by the *Sea*, *Europe* is the lesse, as well as if a *Promontorie* were, as well as if a *Mannor* of thy *friends* or of *thine owne* were; any mans *death* diminishes *me*, because I am involved in *Mankinde;* And therefore never send to know for whom the *bell* tolls; It tolls for *thee*.

JOHN DONNE
Devotions XVII

The Case for Healing

Every thinking person knows that the world is in a mess and extrapolating present trends for merely another ten years results in a horrific picture. Nevertheless, in the hearts of more and more people there is a feeling of optimism – a feeling that beneath the wretched superficial scene momentous divine agencies are at work guiding mankind towards the Right Path. A manifestation of this feeling is the increasing number of people attending seminars and congresses, and joining associations, societies and movements intended to help them develop spiritually. There is increasingly a gut feeling that in our institutions the exercise of wisdom and the expression of intuition vary inversely as the power of computers increases. More and more people realise that our society is indifferent to our earth and its ecology and know that we must face up to our God-given responsibility for the earth and everything on it. It is clear that governments and man-made institutions cannot bring about what needs to be done: the great changes can only come about as the consciousness of millions of men and women expands so that respect for the earth, plant life and animals takes a great leap forward.

This book is intended for people who want to do something positive and constructive to help bring about a more harmonious relationship between people and with our environment. In short, the method is the achievement of increased happiness and expanded consciousness by healing others. It is only in the act of healing that most of us can be certain that our guidance is from God. Now is the time for a great increase in healing activity because new healing

energies are presently being made available to mankind
which enable us to heal adverse conditions, both physical
and non-physical, which to date have been generally intract-
able to the medical profession and all but a few of our
greatest healers. We have to raise our sights beyond physical
ailments and face up to the dis-eases of fear, loneliness and
unhappiness, realms where the medical profession and
social services rarely succeed. Several different methods of
healing are described, two of which almost everyone will be
able to use to good effect.

Essential for the methods of healing described is the use of
the dowser's pendulum. Proper use of the pendulum enables
the dowser to get answers to questions that cannot be
answered by our ordinary consciousness. It is a way of
'finding out' or a method of getting guidance. So, with the
pendulum a water-diviner can 'see' underground water and
a healer can 'see' a diseased organ. The golden rule in
question and answer dowsing is to use the gift only when
there is need. Question and answer dowsing can be used for
many different purposes but here I am mainly concerned
with the use of the pendulum as an aid in healing. Most
people can learn to dowse quite quickly but some may find
they cannot get proper gyrations of the pendulum. Such
people would be well advised not to try to do any healing
until their dowsing is right. The best course of action would
be to get the help of an experienced dowser.

Healing can be of benefit in every home. Parents with
only limited dowsing and healing ability and with little
spare time can do much useful work for their family and
pets by dealing with the minor problems that crop up
frequently. The work harmonises with everyone's daily life
so that one's normal obligations are not neglected. Retired
or unemployed people will find that the work will fill a big
gap. Even only half an hour a day will be sufficient to keep
an eye on diet and remedies for family and pets.

There is nothing supernatural or mysterious about healing. It is happening every day and everywhere. Many people have the gift of proximity healing. When we are in their presence we feel good. Often the effects are transitory, but not infrequently serious physical conditions are cleared as a result of a chance meeting, a handshake or a kiss. It is rare for people who have this gift to be aware of it. Then there is the healing we give out by thinking about other people – friends and relatives and people who have in some measure aroused our sympathy. The nature and power of the healing depend on the individuals' gifts. Here again most people are not aware of these gifts. If they were, they would be able to use them to better advantage.

Apart from the obvious benefits there are greater benefits in the long term. Anyone who undertakes to help others by healing is immediately given the necessary guidance and access to the invisible healing networks, so that people with little healing power can get higher-grade assistance. This means that simple home healing can clear incipient problems which otherwise may not manifest until many years later. The lead time for most types of cancer is as much as forty years, and for most chronic problems twenty to thirty years. Healing at an early age can also clear potential behavioural, mental and emotional problems. Home healing could help to ease the load on the family doctor and in the longer term could ease the load on our hospitals.

In the past forty years or so medicine has made great progress with many diseases but can still do little for the degenerative diseases – where cure can only occur after systemic change – and for conditions not usually regarded as dis-ease such as loneliness and unhappiness, which arise as the result of isolation from our greater environment. Then there is the huge and rapidly growing problem of crime, delinquency and addiction of various kinds which are mostly caused by our 'dirty' environment. In spite of the great progress that has been made in some directions, the National Health Service seems always to be in a state of crisis as the

result of the vast use of increasingly expensive drugs, sophis-
ticated equipment and operations. In an article in *The Daily
Telegraph* in September 1983, Graham Turner quoted some
chilling statistics. He said it was possible to give someone
two new hip-joints and two new knee-joints at a cost of
£35,000. With a finite budget, as the number of these expensive operations increases, so do the waiting-lists for sufferers from hernia, varicose veins and the like. In another
article he said that until recently the annual cost of drugs for
people who had a kidney transplant was £600, but that a
superior drug is now in use costing £3,000 per annum.
Another problem he mentioned was the increase in the
purchase of increasingly expensive equipment. There is no
doubt that drug companies and equipment manufacturers
will continue vigorously to market more expensive products. For thousands of years businessmen have had to
think in terms of cost-effectiveness, but for the medical
profession it is virtually a new concept fraught with agonising decisions for those concerned. In business purchasing is
carefully controlled, with relatively few people having the
authority to buy, whereas in medicine every doctor has the
authority to buy. A consequence of the increasing use of
drugs is the increasing number of people being admitted to
hospital for drug-induced problems. In 1981 there were
100,000 such cases. It is clear that unless something radical is
put in hand there will be a huge crisis in the National Health
Service within a few years.

In mental hospitals, geriatric units, old people's homes,
charitable institutions such as the Cheshire Homes, as well
as in their own homes, are tens of thousands of chronically
ill or senile people having a very poor quality of life and
costing the taxpayer an enormous sum annually in general
care and in drugs. Many are in need of specific dietary
advice which dowsers could give at a distance. Many of
them suffer from allergies which healing could cure. Many
are lonely and would at least gain comfort from the atten-

tions of a healer who may well be able to spend an hour with them at each visit compared with the five minutes a General Practitioner can, on average, give. They are people for whom the medical profession can do little except prescribe surgery or drugs. We can only hope that before long the authorities concerned, and particularly the medical profession, will realise that in cases where they can make no progress it is plain common sense to call in a healer, and downright cruel not to do so. I can speak from the heart on this. I have approached two parsons in the hope that I could do something for their old or chronically ill parishioners, and a lady who runs a home for chronically disadvantaged people, and have met with a blank wall on each occasion.

A fresh problem is the appearance of new diseases such as herpes and AIDS. These are occurring as environmental energies become available which we have not been exposed to for a very long time, and are appearing as the earth's protective cover is changed and as miasms are cleared from people and the ground. The presence of these energies presents, with healing, the opportunity for the sufferers to acquire superior constitutions.

Apart from its role in the health of individuals there are far wider spheres in which only healing can do what is necessary. Much of our industrial relations trouble is caused by people having to work on 'dirty' sites which cause Mind blockages with unreasonable behaviour resulting. Much delinquency and mindless violence similarly are caused by a 'dirty' environment. These problems will progressively decrease as the number of people with Universe Consciousness increases. 'Dirty' waste and agricultural land can be cleaned as the number of people with Cosmic Consciousness increases. Then there are problems on a continental or world scale such as hunger, deforestation, acid rain and the bomb. Right solutions will only be found when there is a great increase in Wisdom throughout the world. The more healers there are, the quicker will these problems be

solved. The cleverness of a few is not enough. It is estimated
that there are around 10,000 healers in this country. With
the interest of individual doctors and sympathetic and
serious treatment from the media this number could increase
to 100,000 in a few years, which would be none too many
for the problems facing us.

   If at this point any reader does not believe in healing as a
reality I suggest he reads David Harvey's splendid book *The
Power to Heal*. The book deals with some of the great healers
in history, starting with Hippocrates, and goes on to the
methods and results of some of our great present-day healers. One passage about Clive Harris filled me with awe. In
November 1981 Harris made a three-week tour of Poland
with the support of the Roman Catholic Church and the
approval of the Communist Party, taking in eighteen cities.
Crowds of up to 15,000 people gathered day after day in the
bitter cold, waiting to file past and be touched by the healer.
To get through his schedule he worked from six in the
morning until twelve at night. In all it was estimated he
treated about 300,000 people, many of whom reported
cures. Among other things, what he was doing was clearing
fear and shame from their Beings, thus permitting Universe
love to enter.

   Would-be healers should not be intimidated by the technical passages of this book. Very soon most people will be
able to do useful work on diets and the use of simple
remedies. Some of the healing methods are very simple and
can be used by almost anyone including aged and ailing
people. Parkinson's law applies in this healing regime.
Work tends to expand to fill the time available so that those
who really wish to do good healing and have the time will
discover that they soon master the more advanced and
technical aspects and will find themselves breaking new
ground when every working session becomes an adventure.

Dowsing Leads to Healing

Looking back I can see that my involvement with healing began in 1946 during a visit to Ireland when my brother-in-law introduced me to dowsing with a hazel rod. I found that I got an immediate reaction and was able to dowse for water. However I was busy at the office and it never occurred to me to try to become a successful water-diviner. My imagination had however been fired, and I read all the books I could find on the subject. Quite soon I could perform parlour tricks with a wooden pendulum, which I was able to use in a variety of ways.

The first useful application came about in 1949 when I heard that a gang of men in St. Ives had been digging for several days trying to find an electricity cable. I was unable to go there myself so I made up a pendulum with an india-rubber and a piece of string, and showed an engineer in the office how to use it. He went to St. Ives and immediately located the cable. Another little job I remember from those days was for a friend who managed an estate at St. Germans. A hilly meadow was flooding and, assuming that the drains were laid in herringbone formation, men had started digging to find the blockage. After three days of fruitless work my friend asked me if I could help. With the pendulum I traced the drains and found the layout was zigzag. I was able to locate the blockage within half an hour. That little job gave me great satisfaction.

In 1954 my wife and I went with a farmer friend to visit his son's farm situated above the Tamar on the Cornish side, and we were told how a lady had map dowsed an underground stream before going on site to pin-point the place to drill. She told him that they would have to drill eighty feet and the water would rise to within ten feet of the surface. And so it did. I took to map dowsing like a duck to water and for years afterwards I spent many hours looking for underground water, archaeological remains and missing bits of Roman roads. I remember one incident that astonished me. I was searching for Roman roads in the Midlands when I found that I had crossed the Fosse Way without getting a positive pendulum reaction. On enquiring I discovered that the Fosse Way as we know it today was a Roman development of a road that was constructed 8,000 years ago. My first useful map dowsing job was for a friend in Cornwall when we were living near Bristol. He was having a bungalow built in the garden of his house and the waterworks people were unable to find the main. He sent me a sketch and I was able to dowse that the main actually ran through his garden. The big problem with much of the map dowsing I was doing in those years was that it was impossible to verify much of the work. I now know that that unverified map dowsing had a purpose. I was making, superconsciously, the acquaintance of Devas, Universe spirits who have territorial responsibilities.

In the late 1960s when I was Chief Engineer of the South Western Electricity Board it occurred to me that it should be possible to locate faults and weaknesses on electricity distribution and transmission systems. My engineers were very sceptical but the one or two jobs they fed to me I was able to deal with successfully. One job I vividly remember was sent to me by an engineer at our research establishment at Capenhurst. He sent me the cable plan of a housing estate on which there was a cable fault the local engineers could not locate without resorting to 'cut and carve' which is very expensive. There was no indication where the estate was. I made a successful fix and learned subsequently that it was near Liverpool.

After I retired I became interested for a time in locating oil leaks on 33,000 volt cables. At that time the only way to find leaks was by digging holes in the ground and inspecting the cable. As they are usually about three feet down and many of the runs are in excess of 10,000 yards long, finding and repairing leaks was very expensive. I was asked to investigate, by map dowsing, a slow leak on a cable in Devon. I made a fix and as this was my first attempt at that type of work I asked Bill Lewis, a great dowser and healer, to check my fix. He did so and agreed with my location but said there was a weakness on a section of the cable beyond that shown on the map I had been given, and that the cable would fail within three months if it was not attended to in the meantime. I got another route map and located the weakness and agreed with Bill's estimate of time to failure. Our estimate was wrong: the cable failed at the indicated spot within eleven weeks. I was then asked to investigate a leak on a 33,000 volt cable in Croydon, and successfully located it to within ten yards on the 8,000 yard run. Two subsequent jobs were failures and that was the end of that! The feeling amongst the engineers concerned seemed to be that if you succeed in the impossible once it is a fluke, and if you cannot do the impossible all the time you are a phony. After that I was able to prove beyond doubt that it was possible to scan large sections of rural distribution systems and pinpoint weaknesses that needed attention. In the mid 1950s, at a large rural substation in Devon before thirty professional engineers, I had been able to locate the runs of all the underground cables emanating from the site. My various efforts to get my own and other engineers interested in applying dowsing and map dowsing to their work were, so far as I know, totally unsuccessful. It does seem that, for most people, a professional training has the effect of blocking the imagination.

In the early 1970s I saw two programmes on the TV which made a big impression on me. The first concerned Clive Harris who was being 'tested' by a panel of experts under the chairmanship of Magnus Magnusson. Harris had offered to try to heal any subject the BBC would care to bring before him. The subject they produced was a middle-aged man whose fists had been clenched for some years. The healer stroked the man's hands for a minute or two whereupon his fists opened up, and as he opened and closed his hands tears streamed down his face. When asked to comment a doctor on the panel pathetically said that whilst he agreed function had improved he did not think there had been a cure. The other programme, A Leap in the Dark, featured Linda Blandford who was being given an examination by the healer Bill Lewis. She lay on a table whilst Bill examined her body using a pendulum. I think that he discovered about a dozen adverse conditions such as strained eye-muscles and fluid on a lung. It subsequently needed three or four specialists to check his diagnosis with the result that ten of the conditions were agreed and two or three were unproven. Although, no doubt like thousands of other viewers, I was impressed and amazed, no positive thoughts or calls to action came to my mind: my unconscious however had noted and remembered these events.

In the winter of 1975 my wife was in great pain with gall-bladder trouble. She went to the doctor who suggested that she should see a surgeon. She was not happy at the thought of an operation so, from a list of radionic practitioners, I dowsed the name of a lady in London. My wife wrote to her and she was sent a homoeopathic remedy. Within two or three weeks the problem had cleared up. The cost then was about £3.

In the spring of 1976 I was taking our dog, Jill, for a walk when I said something like this – "How the devil do you expect us to find the right path through life?" That was the moment I was 'hooked' on healing. Shortly after that I was browsing at a bookstall at a healing conference when I saw a little book on the Essenes. I knew I had to buy it and at what page to open it. It was a little prayer asking to be kept on the Right Path.

It was also about that time I was introduced to healing by Bill Lewis. During our talk I mentioned the subject of radionics. This is a method of distant healing with the aid of diagnostic and healing apparatus. The basis of this healing is to make a diagnosis in the form of a series of numbers and then find another series for the healing which is then transmitted with the aid of the apparatus. Bill told me that I could heal that way, without the need for apparatus, by dowsing the remedial series of numbers with the pendulum. The next day I had my first patient, a golfing friend. He had been smitten with a terrible depression, something he had suffered from before on several occasions. Sometimes it lasted for three or four weeks. After I had phoned him and discovered that he was ill, I sat down and worked out a remedial series. Half an hour later he telephoned to say he felt fine and suggested a game of golf. Afterwards he said he had never felt better and he has had no recurrence of the problem. I realise now that by dowsing the number series I had asked for the help of the right healing spirit for that particular problem.

I was not allowed to use the number method of healing again; instead when distant healing I worked to the model of seven etheric bodies each with seven chakras. When hand healing I would, with the aid of the pendulum, find out where to place my hands, and for how long. Diet and remedies, of course, I examined with the pendulum. Although my range was limited my physical healing was quite good. Things went very well until the autumn of 1977 when I woke up one morning feeling very odd, rather disembodied. I never thought of seeing a doctor; instead I went to see that fine and well-known healer, Rose Gladden. She spent about two hours on me, mostly hand healing my head. When I was leaving she said if I ever needed her help I could telephone her day or night. She put me on an even keel; I lost the disembodied feeling, but when the next day I began to do my distant healing I found that I had lost most of my healing powers. Instead of giving physical healing as before I had to heal levels of consciousness, understanding, knowledge and perception which led to brain and systemic change. Therefore often, instead of giving quick relief, I had to heal in a much more complex manner, because every healing was involving the etheric bodies, brain, systems and organs. In my own case five systems began to change to superior modes as blocks were cleared.

My hand healing powers similarly had gone but instead I was given the gift of touch healing for clearing a big range of allergies and for putting systemic change in train. This is accomplished by lightly touching the hands, face, neck and feet of a patient with my fingers or part of the hand. When working in this way my hands and fingers know exactly where to go and what to do without conscious thought. I also found later that I had been given very powerful proximity healing powers. These became available when my Universe body began to function properly. With this gift I was able to clear the way so that healing spirits could get through to my patients. Invariably they worked on the Cosmic Body which I was unable to help with my own powers. Another new gift was the ability, when distant or proximity healing, to call in healing friends to help when necessary.

Shortly after this turning-point in my healing I found that I was being taught by a number of discarnate and incarnate friends, and that I was being given new knowledge. The most important guidance was that everyone had potentially available ten etheric bodies each with ten chakras and ten levels of consciousness. At the same time I was taught the method of using the pendulum for the advanced healing work described in this book. This can be put very simply in these words: "It doesn't matter what the problem is, nor how it came about, just find out what to do now." Thus, diagnosis became irrelevant. I never researched or tried to find out anything as an objective. As I made progress in my practical healing work I was given information which resulted in this book.

Dowsing for Healing

Man has used the gift of dowsing for many thousands of years to find water, minerals and buried objects using a forked stick, and today throughout the world there are many professional and amateur dowsers using their dowsing skill for many different purposes. Early this century dowsing took a great step forward as a result of the work of the Abbé Mermet, a French priest who practised dowsing with a pendulum over a period of forty years. His book *Principles and Practice of Radiesthesia,* published in 1935, is a classic and gives many case histories of the location of water, minerals and natural gas and of healing. Unlike many pioneers he was honoured in his lifetime and was commended by the Pope for his great achievements. For the majority of people wishing to learn and practise holistic healing the ability to use the pendulum is essential. As well as enabling the operator to perceive physical objects not visible to the eye it enables him to detect fields, radiations and spirits which cannot be detected by conventional technology. Furthermore it is an invaluable aid in self-learning.

Pendulums are available in perspex, plastic, steel and wood. The wooden pendulum is the best for most people. For beginners the first step is to learn the question and answer technique. Hold the pendulum between the thumb and forefinger of the right hand with about three inches of free thread and make it oscillate gently to and fro; then ask mentally for the pendulum to indicate 'yes'. For most people it will begin to gyrate in a clockwise direction. For 'no' the gyration will be anti-clockwise. The next step is to make a list of foods and beverages; by pointing to the individual items with a pen or pencil held in the left hand, and noting the pendulum gyration, you will find out which you can 'perceive'. At first you may not be able to 'see' more than half the items but with practice your performance should soon improve. Then learn to 'see' the vital organs. You should then be able to do useful work by checking your diet and that of your family and friends. Another valuable exercise is to learn to 'see' different subsoils, limestone, coal, clay etc.

After that you should learn to map dowse. There are two main purposes for map dowsing for healing; to find point features such as energy centres and to find linear tracks which could be ley lines of some sort, underground water or energy routes. For the former, with the pendulum held in the right hand, bring your pencil down the left-hand margin of the map until you get a positive gyration and then move your pencil to the right until you get another positive gyration: you should then have located your target. For linear features traverse the map with the pendulum until you get a positive gyration, then follow the track.

The most important point features you need to be able to locate are energy, cleansing and healing centres. Within a radius of thirty miles from your home you should be able to pin-point centres for the ten main fields. People can often benefit from visiting these centres. If it is indicated for a patient you will usually find that a visit to the indicated cleansing centre should take place first, so that redundant elements of the Being can be cleared; this may be followed the same day by a visit to the appropriate healing centre so that new elements can be picked up. The pendulum will indicate the right day for the visit. Other point features to be detected are animal and human remains. The probability is that associated with such remains will be etheric bodies in need of healing. If, as will usually be the case with beginners, you are unable to heal them, you should be able to locate their position and if necessary clear beds or favourite chairs from directly above them. Many problems are caused by streams running underneath houses. If they are offensive it is because of the presence of animal or human bodies upstream. If you are unable to cleanse them the remedy again is to move any favourite chairs or beds from directly above them. A valuable dowsing gift is the ability to call for help 'over the air' from your 'fellow-workers'.

The ability to dowse is a very great gift, given to us to make life easier. Many people have the gift but sadly many misuse it by asking inappropriate, ambiguous or silly questions. It should only be used if there is need. An example of a wrong question is if a golfer, before leaving for his golf-course, were to ask "is it going to rain?" It would be the wrong question because it would not be asking for simple guidance. The right question would be "should I take my umbrella and waterproofs with me this afternoon?" Some dowsers can use the pendulum for ascertaining 'truth' – for example to ask if a bank statement is correct – but for our present purpose I am only concerned with the dowsing techniques needed for healing.

Obtaining Higher Guidance

So far I have been dealing with simple dowsing which is not adequate for getting the guidance which is needed for breaking new ground. Until about five years ago I believed that in working with the pendulum the conscious mind posed the question and the intuition, via the pendulum, gave the answer, yes or no; and when working alone my distant healing and my learning were based on this method. However, I gradually realised that the method was limited, in that the questions could only be based on concepts already in the dowser's ordinary consciousness or available to him on paper. How then could the dowser get true inspiration? The answer I found was that both the question and the answer must come from the intuition, that is from one or more of the levels of consciousness or perception. In this way one can be given guidance and information which were previously inconceivable. The golden rule whenever doing other than simple dowsing with a pendulum, at any point in time, is that there is only one question to be asked and the imagination must discover it. This is not as difficult as it may appear. I can usually find the right question within a few shots. The second rule for success is to take careful note of the movement of the pendulum. If it is anything other than a smooth gyration it means that the question is incorrect or imprecise, the timing is wrong, or that the mind is busy with other work.

Anyone attempting to use this method would be wise to write at the top of his notepad the instructions: go, wait, use more imagination, finish and 'drop it'. This last injunction is important because by this method one is not trying to do this or that; one is being guided on the right path that will give the optimum benefit for the patient in the overall context. The area of search is so wide because the healing is holistic. We are dealing to the best of our ability with the whole being, which is involved with every form of life, including forms we usually regard as inanimate, because, as Paracelsus said, "all form has spirit, but not all spirit has form." Another concept for which I am indebted to Paracelsus is 'the hour in time.' Just as there is a time to sow seeds so there is a time at which to heal each patient. A healer working in this way will find that the pendulum will give the appropriate time and date for each healing appointment. It is fairly unusual to find that one begins by dealing with the patient who has asked for help. More often one will initially be guided to direct one's thoughts to a relative of the patient, his house, or to the ground on which his house stands. The one certain thing is that the healer's field of enquiry will be much wider than with most types of healing. For example, four times out of five, when dealing with a pet or a domestic animal, it is the owner who is in need of healing.

Some people may find it difficult to see why the method I have described is necessary. Perhaps this explanation will help. Many dowsers do good healing work by making a diagnosis, in medical terms, with the aid of the pendulum. They then seek to discover the appropriate course of action and remedies. It is clear that for both processes they have been getting guidance from some higher intelligence. However, for both the diagnosis and the subsequent action they are relying on knowledge already in their minds or available on paper. It seems to make sense to leave the entire problem to the higher intelligence; forget the process of diagnosis and by asking at each step "what shall I do now?" find out what has to be done by thought or action. I hope that experienced dowser-healers using the diagnostic approach do not feel that in the above remarks I am belittling their efforts; far from it. Any good healer is receiving guidance from higher intelligences and for some of them the method I have described may be unhelpful or unnecessary, but it will help beginners to make speedier progress than would otherwise be the case.

This is my normal way of working when on my own or with a patient who happens to be a sensitive, or when I am leading a workshop with a group of people. Often at the start of such a session I am told what the objective is, which may be the commissioning of a chakra or a level of consciousness, or clearing an ancient miasm in the ground somewhere. It may be anything. A session may last up to two hours and the objective can only be attained by giving distant or hand healing to patients. Each significant step forward comes only after work. Apart from the benefits to patients and other distant targets there is also benefit to the healer in the way of increased sensitivity, extended awareness and an increased depth and range of healing powers. In this way I have worked with many healers in many countries whom I have never met and whose names I do not know. Working with discarnate friends is no different from working with distant incarnate friends.

For Beginners

Anyone wishing to start healing would be well advised to work with a friend or in a small group. Progress will be much swifter than starting off on one's own. The first thing to learn is how to 'see' different foods with the pendulum. This can be done by looking at an item of food or drink on a list by pointing the left forefinger at the item, and with the pendulum held in the right hand asking if you can 'see' it. Probably at first there will be quite a number of foods that you cannot 'see' but with practice your dowsing will soon improve. The next stage is then to learn to 'see' nutritional supplements and vitamins. After that you should begin to work on the model, asking which of your own subtle bodies, chakras and levels of consciousness you can 'see'. When you have made some progress with this you can begin to look at the dietary needs of members of your group and interested friends. At first you will probably only be able to examine the diet of people in your company but quite soon, as your sensitivity and intuition improve, you will be able to advise distant friends on diet and simple remedies.

The next step within your group is to learn touch and hand healing. You can find where your fingers or hands have to be applied by scanning the body with the left forefinger, with the pendulum held in the right hand. The duration of each treatment can be discovered by asking whether it is one minute, two minutes and so on. Sooner or later you will find your hands and fingers will know exactly what to do without need for the pendulum, and the work will be accomplished much more quickly. The first essays in distant work could be for members of the group to 'look' at each other when they are apart. It may well be that you will be able to 'see' more of each other's dietary needs than when you were together. When the group has attained reasonable proficiency in the above work a start can be made by the group as a whole giving distant healing to interested and sympathetic members of their families or friends. Progress will be very much quicker if you can get the help of a skilled dowser-healer.

In this healing regime no great knowledge of anatomy or physiology is needed. Initially most healers will only be able to use simple dowsing, but as their awareness expands and as their skill increases they will be able to get guidance from higher intelligences by working on the basis of 'what shall I do now?' Many will then find they are being helped to break new ground in areas such as 'women's problems', senility and loneliness. When this phase begins they will get help from their 'fellow-workers' (healers) which will speed up their work. At a later stage they will get help from specialist networks and later still from the holistic healing network.

Dowsers can get a lot of pleasure from map and on site dowsing for underground streams, miasms, archaeological sites, energy centres etc. Some using the question and answer method will be able to work out the depths at which artefacts, streams and sub-soil strata can be found. Many will have the gift of psychometry, that is of dating objects and finding out something about their history. This sort of work, as well as being a source of pleasure, will speed up the acquisition of new perceptions which will be of benefit in healing work.

Apart from highly specialised disciplines such as chiropractic, acupuncture, hypnotherapy etc., which call for extensive study and training, there are a number of different schools employing different methods of distant and hand healing. If a beginner considers joining some such body he would be wise first to become a reasonably proficient dowser because this would provide a firm basis for his future development and would enable him to keep an eye on his own needs and progress. A beginner healer who cannot dowse is like a man walking through a dark wood at night without a torch. In the British Society of Dowsers are many good healers. Most of them are self-taught and they use every imaginable method and technique. Any beginner would do well to ask the Secretary for advice. Details of the Society are given at the back of the book.

The Possible Human Being

At birth human consitutions vary greatly because of different experiences in former incarnations, for ancestral reasons and because of the circumstances of conception and birth. As we get older we are exposed to new experiences, to illness, to joys and sorrows. Then there are the normal ageing processes. From this it seems probable to me that our illnesses and unhappiness relate more to our constitution than to a specific germ, virus or event. There are big constitutional differences at birth between different races and between individuals within one race. We do not begin life all equal; we are all unique and born with different gifts and potentials.

To the conventional medical mind we are largely physical bodies to be treated, although psychology and psychiatry exist as methods of dealing with what are judged to be non-physical problems. To the healer, however, a human being is spirit and body, not separate but united. Every physical element of the body from a cell to, say, a bone, to be healthy must be partnered by the appropriate spirit or, put another way, there are physical correspondences to our spirit elements.

Man has available ten etheric bodies which are responsible for our functioning, viz our physical processes, our thoughts and actions. In the Bible there are references to seven such bodies, and the Indian beliefs, which have been the basis for much Western esoteric thinking, also refer to seven bodies. There is no doubt that Christ and some of his disciples had ten etheric bodies working well because only such a constitution could account for their great healing powers which seem to us to have been miraculous. Our greatest healers today, regardless of their religious persuasions, have ten bodies working well. These bodies are our interfaces with the great Spirits of the Universe which are the concern of man. When we are able to perceive – that is know – these Spirits, we are given gifts. Our etheric bodies have, of course, many roles. For our present purpose we are only concerned with those involved in providing energies for functioning and for levels of consciousness, understanding, knowledge and perception. These levels control our thoughts and actions. The etheric bodies corresponding to the great Spirits with which mankind is concerned are:- Earth, Air, Water, Sun, Nature, Mind, Soul, Spirit, Cosmic and Universe. Each etheric body has ten chakras.

For the generation of vitalities which we need for functioning the bodies relate to parts of the brain, body tissues and systems; levels of consciousness relate to the fingers and toes, and non–physical perceptions relate to fingernails and toenails. The functions relate to the ten vital organs and glands.

The bodies can be regarded as top managers, the levels of consciousness as senior managers and the chakras as process managers. The Chairman and Chief Executive is God, but all too often he is unable to take over many elements of the Being which have to manage as best they can.

It was about four years ago that I was able to name the ten bodies, but it was only recently I was able to get some confirmation of them from a little book *The Gospel of Peace of Jesus Christ* published by C.W. Daniel. This is a translation by Edmond Szekely of the original Aramaic text recording Christ's healing teaching written by his beloved disciple, John. Christ tells his audience that they must first know their Earth Mother. Then, amongst some very practical advice on diet and hygiene, he refers to the Air, Water and Sun in that order as personified spirits. In the foreword Szekely says of Christ "And though his words, as we have them today in the New Testament, have been terribly mutilated and deformed, they nevertheless have conquered half of humanity and the whole of the civilisation of the West. This fact proves the eternal vitality of the Master's words, and their supreme and incomparable value."

THE SYSTEMS

The ten systems are shown below, together with their corresponding body tissues.

Digestive	Skeleton
Respiration	Cartilage
Defecation	Suspensory ligaments and tendons
Lymph	Muscles
Genital	Flesh
Urinary	Organs
Cardio-Vascular-Circulation	Ducts
Para-sympathetic Nervous	Membranes
Sympathetic Nervous	Nerves
Central Nervous	Skin

The environmental fields working on the body tissues and systems generate the vitalities which are needed for the functions and are carried to the brain by connective tissues. These vitalities can be provided by the metabolism but it is rare for more than half of them to be provided in this manner. For the vast majority of people only nine vitalities are available from the environmental fields because, for the generation of vitalities, digestion and defecation constitute one system, and the lymph system is only partially operative. Because of these constitutional defects six vitalities are weak – Spirit, Nature, Air, Universe, Sun and Cosmic. These vitalities are needed for powering the levels of consciousness, understanding, knowledge and perception and, in conjunction with the appropriate glands, for physical functioning. Thus it is possible for people to be sensitive and intelligent and have good morale even if their physical condition is poor.

THE FUNCTIONS

The ten functions are shown below, together with their corresponding vital organs and glands.

1 Energy generation and distribution – stomach and parathyroids
This includes the generation and distribution of energy in the form of blood.

2 Physical senses, perceptions and control – lungs and pineal gland

3 Elimination – bowel and adenoids
This includes the lymph system, ejaculation, perspiration and the elimination of toxins and disease residues.

4 Muscular activity and co-ordination – spleen and adrenal glands
This affects all proper muscular activity, such as location of organs, posture, movement and physical skills.

5 Sexual activity – gall bladder and ovaries or testes
Its role is obvious, but with the superior constitution the act of love becomes a much superior experience.

6 Thinking – kidneys and tonsils
This involves perceptions, common sense – a quite rare attribute – thinking, imagination, reason, inspiration and, most rare, wisdom.

7 Healing – heart and thymus
This concerns proximity, distant, touch and hand healing of humans, animals, plants and trees.

8 Cleansing – pancreas and thyroid gland
This involves the internal and external cleansing of humans, animals, plants and trees, and organic and inorganic substances, of miasms, bad influences and products of man-made aggression.

9 Energising – liver and pituitary gland
This brings into service elements of the Being after healing and cleansing have been affected.

10 Protection – brain and hypothalamus
This means of the whole Being by proper functioning of the hypothalamus and perception of the environmental spirits with which we are concerned.

It is notable that some of the vital organs and glands are often regarded as being of little importance by the medical profession: but loss of any of these means that some functioning is impaired. The Being, however, always makes the best of a bad job so that, if a life function is in danger, less vital functions will whenever possible be sacrificed.

The constitution as described does not conform to the traditional view but is more comprehensive as it demonstrates what I know to be true – that everyone has the latter four functions working to some extent and that they are part of man's proper constitution. They cannot be comprehended by the conventional medical mind, embodying as they do non-physical and subtle elements. They can only be apprehended by a sensitive or a dowser if his Universe Body and Perceptions 3 and 4 are in service.

THE LEVELS OF CONSCIOUSNESS AND PERCEPTION

The main levels of consciousness are the ten etheric bodies. When these are associated with the appropriate part of the brain there is consciousness; that is the etheric body has its proper relationship with the great Spirit. Under each main level of consciousness there are ten sub-levels. They are:

1 Obligations
2 Needs
3 Family and friends
4 Fellow-workers
5 Sexual partners
6 Perceptions, intuition and dowsing
7 Patients
8 Brothers and sisters for support of levels of consciousness, understanding, knowledge and perception
9 Right path
10 Future

Also associated with each main level of consciousness are ten perceptions. They are:

1 Inanimate physical environment
2 Virus and germs
3 Plants and trees
4 Insects, animals and humans
5 Diet and remedies
6 Physical senses
7 Fields, healing centres and energies
8 Spirits
9 Plants, trees, animals and humans in need of help
10 Other healers and healing networks

Our thoughts and actions in any situation depend on our consciousness and perceptions to open the appropriate chakras for conscious functioning. Most of our bodily functions are unconscious, in that they are under Divine control, but most of our problems stem from our ordinary consciousness which is mostly under the control of what I can only describe as a middle self. As right path healing proceeds, more and more of our thoughts and actions become subject to Divine guidance and life becomes very different. Needless to say, for most of us our consciousness and perceptions are inadequate and chaotic. The average man of fifty in this country has consciousness of only three or four main levels. Thus, apart from our physical well-being, we are very poorly equipped to face life. The dominant body for functioning is the Cosmic Body, but for a lot of people this is in a very poor state so that many of that body's functions have to be taken on as best can be by other bodies. As the paramount consideration is always to preserve life, it is the higher functions which suffer most. Gifts, such as the ability to drive a car, play good golf or be a good musician are controlled by the Universe Body.

To a clairvoyant a possible human being would resemble a cross between a Christmas-tree and a firework display because of the auras and emanations of various types. The auras are the interfaces between the great Spirits and our etheric bodies. There would be beams for distant healing, emissions for proximity healing, radiations for protection, and a magnetic field for protecting us from psychic aggression. Every subtle energy, whether generated from an incoming environmental field, or from the digestion of food should have a corresponding output from the skin.

Energy and Healing Centres and Influences

Over the surface of the earth and the sea bed are innumerable energy centres which provide the subtle energies all forms of life need for proper functioning. Some, but not all, of these energies can be provided by the digestion of food. These centres are linked by a network of ley lines from which run distrbutors to make the energies available to all forms of animal and plant life. There are, as well, healing and cleansing centres also linked by ley lines with distributors making their energies available to healers. The interconnectors and distributors are often blocked by miasms which are etheric elements of humans and animals in need of healing. Some of these miasms are very old, belonging to animals and types of man long extinct. It is becoming increasingly possible for them to be cleared as new energy and healing centres are established. Five years ago for a time I consciously participated with a Universe spirit in establishing new centres, but now in my participation, like that of many others, takes place without conscious effort. The main energy centres of the earth are located as follows:

Earth	Zaire
Air	Yosemite, California
Water	Karnak, Egypt
Sun	Heliopolis (Baalbek), Lebanon
Nature	Kandy, Sri Lanka
Mind	Mount Everest
Soul	Glastonbury
Spirit	Peking
Cosmic	Peru
Universe	Jerusalem

In this country the most powerful places are ancient sites such as Glastonbury, Avebury, Iona, Stonehenge and some of our cathedrals and spas. Certain of them can be identified by stone circles and standing stones but many have been overbuilt. They are healing centres established by our forebears at various times in prehistory. Dowsers will be able to identify the energies emanating from them. When in use they were carefully guarded to ensure that the only people admitted were those for whom exposure to the fields would be beneficial. The earliest sites were for Earth energy followed by Nature. As long as 10,000 years ago there were centres for all the ten bodies. As time passed, life on earth became exposed to new fields, usually with harmful effect. In time, however, after each new exposure, man learned how to heal so that life was enriched. Up to about 200 years ago in this country we intuitively avoided building on such sites, on 'dirty' miasmic sites and on burial grounds, but since then our intuition hasbecome progressively weaker in this and in other respects, with the result that many people at home, at work or perhaps in hospital, are in a harmful environment. In our society most affected is Mind. Many people could do themselves a lot of good if they were to visit a suitable site which could as well be a housing estate as Iona. These sites can be discovered by map dowsing. Problems can also arise from the subsoil and from underground water. It is convenient to mention here another source of trouble which I refer to as 'bad influences'. They are created by negative thoughts and emotions and remain in situ until they are cleansed by humans or animals.

In recent years there has been a vast increase in the number of healing centres – in this country tenfold. All Sainsbury's stores are now Spirit centres; government, local authority premises and the like are Mind centres; many churches and other places of worship are Soul centres; golf-courses and sports areas are Earth centres and parks and woodlands etc. are Nature centres. Therefore, whether we like it or not, all of us, every day, are being exposed to energies we may not have been exposed to for a very long time. The fact that there are so few adverse effects following on this real increase in energy availability is due to the existence of the holistic healing network in which all life is represented and which, under Divine direction, dispenses healing without the conscious participation of mankind. Even so, new problems and illnesses will follow and it will be unfortunate if those responsible for the nation's welfare and for the media disregard it. Any dowser having Universe Consciousness and Perception 7 working (fields, energy centres and energies) will be able to locate all or some of them if he wishes to do so.

A problem well-known to dowsers is that of 'black streams'. These are caused by miasms upstream of the property and can have a debilitating effect on people living or working over them and can also cause serious illness. Dowsers have helped many people by locating the course of such streams thus enabling the sufferer to move his chair or bed out of the way. Many dowsers have also done good work and diverted the miasm by driving iron rods into the ground at positions indicated by the pendulum or rod. The best way of dealing with them however is by healing them. As well as being bad for humans and animals they are bad for crops and plants growing above them. A large part of the surface of the earth is adversely affected by them. Poor land can be greatly improved by clearing miasms and bad influences.

The main reason we are vulnerable to bad influences and miasms is because most of us are short of nerves; the circuit shortfall is made up as best can be by non-physical connections, like little radio links, which are in part external to the body. Often in the presence of bad influences some of these non-physical connections are broken. Most of them begin to function again when we move away from the offending influences, but sometimes they remain disconnected. This can result in long term depression and loss of vitality. Throughout life the firm channels (the nerves) are reserved for vital functions, the more fragile links having to serve for higher sensory functions. If a person receives the right healing, which may be just by visiting a particular place or being in the proximity of the right person, or by more formal healing, over the years the number of properly functioning nerves may increase dramatically.

Digestion, Metabolism and Skin

Many animals live happily on a diet of grass; eskimos, we are told, could live on a diet of seal-meal and fish; peasants in the East can perform very arduous manual work on a meagre diet of rice and some fruit and vegetables. In this country some people live well on a frugal vegetarian diet. Why is it, then, we are told by nutritional experts that we need a varied diet, that we should not eat sugar and that salt and fats are bad for us?

There must be a reason why we have to be so careful about diet. Looked at in the light of this theory of environmental energies, the answer is simple. Compared with us these people and animals living a simpler life and having a good cleansing function are able to make better use of these energies which, for our purpose now, have two main roles; they are needed for good functioning and, in conjunction with a superior digestion, they can provide physical energy.

When considering digestive and metabolic problems it is instructive to look at our major remedies – tea, coffee, nicotine and alcohol – in relation to the subtle energies. Our dependence on tea stems from lack of certain energies from Nature, Water, Air and Sun; for coffee, Nature, Sun and Air; for nicotine, Nature, Air, Earth and Soul, and for alcohol, Universe, Cosmic, Nature and Mind. The need for hard and soft drugs results from imbalances in the Universe Body. This shows where our main subtle energy deficiencies lie.

It is often said that man is what he eats. This is usually untrue. If the digestion and metabolism are in bad shape, diet is critical, but for people with good digestive and metabolic functions this ceases to be so. Their main need is to take in enough energy food for physical functioning.

Most dowsers using the model will be able to dowse diets that will improve the sense of well-being and often speed up physical repairs. A few examples may be helpful, starting with the Universe Body. If it is in bad shape it may be found that white bread should be eliminated from the diet. Problems with the Cosmic Body are often exacerbated by meat. Fruit and fruit juices can provoke adverse conditions of the Water Body, similarly potatoes can cause trouble if the state of the Nature Body is poor. The above are quoted as examples; most dowsers will be able to give precise advice on all the bodies. The main thing to bear in mind is that we are all unique, and that specific diets such as are often given in magazines and books are a nonsense. One man's meat is another's poison.

Some people, whilst experiencing no actual discomfort, have poor digestions in that they are unable to extract essential trace elements from their food. This is usually caused by the lack of a digestive secretion from the pancreas which can follow an attack of glandular fever, an ailment many people have without experiencing any marked symptoms. The functions that suffer most are physical stamina, and protection against adverse ground radiations. Another secretion that sometimes fails for the same reason is one from the gall-bladder to the stomach. The result is people are unable to digest bread completely, which has an adverse effect on sexuality.

People should not lightly decide to become vegetarians: certainly not on moral grounds alone. The metabolism of most of us in the Western world is such that we need some meat. To be in really good health on a vegetarian diet a digestive secretion from the spleen is needed. In this country only about one person in twenty has this secretion, whereas in India almost everyone has it. For many, lack of meat results in lowered physical energy and mental stamina. When people are ill or convalescent an adequate meat intake is vital, as this is the best food for providing the energies for the physical repairs that are always necessary. In the old days beef-tea was the norm for sick people, but I never hear of it these days.

We all know people who have a tremendous appetite but remain slim, and others who are overweight on a very light diet. This being so, it is odd that so many with a weight problem think only of going on a rigorous diet which probably provides inadequate subtle energies for proper functioning. On the radio I heard a pathetic little story which illustrates this point. A woman who had achieved a massive weight reduction was being interviewed. The interviewer asked if she was happy about the result. "Oh", she said, "I am very happy but I haven't the strength to clean my windows now." There are three main reasons why people become overweight; from water retention due to a poor kidney function, from fat accumulation to give protection when that given by the hypothalamus fails, and because a thyroid secretion has failed. There is no simple remedy.

I recently bought a little book on diet, which is intended to be a simple guide for the man in the street. The text is brief and sensible but then there is a set of tables giving the protein, fat, carbohydrate and calorific content of seven hundred different foods and drinks. I shudder to think what was the cost of the laboratory work involved in the production of the tables. It is clear that such a mass of information could not possibly be of any real help to anyone wanting to check on or improve his diet. Anyone seriously trying to use it would probably end up in a state of neurosis. We have been told that potatoes are bad for us, now we are told they are good. We were told that bran was good for us with the result that many people made themselves ill with the stuff; now some experts do not like the idea of people eating bran; they believe we should get sufficient roughage from wholemeal bread and vegetables. We are told that salt is bad for us, that sugar is bad, that fat is bad and so on *ad nauseum*. When living in Cornwall we had a farmer friend who was regard-ed by everyone who knew him as a 'lovely' man. He was very kind, a progressive farmer and a good father. Since his youth his basic alcohol intake had been one gallon of his own potent cider a day and when he went out for a drink he would take anything offered to him. His favourite tipple was gin and whisky mixed. He had enjoyed good health and died in his late seventies having had a great and happy life. Without the alcohol he would have soon died because his Cosmic Body was totally lacking in its natural protection. It is clear that nutritionists are all at sea and will continue to be so until they realise that man is more than a machine.

If anyone is born with a defective digestive function or the function has been impaired by disease the function cannot be improved by conventional medicine: it can only be put right by a healer having Universe consciousness and sub level of consciousness 10 in operation. The main diseases which impair the digestion are measles, german measles and glandular fever which can block a secretion from the pancreas. The innoculations against these diseases have the same effect. Many poisons can also impair the digestion. Even if right healing is given it may be many months or years before the systemic change is complete; in the meantime, lecithin, ginseng, honey and yeast tablets will be very beneficial.

The skin is a vital organ, and hair too vitally important. For a good metabolism hair and skin should admit the beneficial energies and reject the undesirable ones. In the Western world very little Air, Sun and Nature get through. The result is poor metabolism and lowered vitality. The most important areas are the head, cheeks, hands and feet, because it is in these areas that vital subtle energies and sensory impressions should be received. They are important for the sensory, control and protective functions, and block-ages in these areas can lead to chronic metabolic and digestive problems. Women tend to be more affected than men because of their use of cosmetics and body sprays which can cause blockages. Moreover, some people are allergic to certain preparations without being aware of it. There is also the problem that some elements of these preparations may be absorbed into the tissues. For any adverse condition it is important to check for such problems. Often people using unsuitable preparations can be shown alternative popular brands, but sometimes for people with a very sensitive skin it will be necessary to recommend herbal-based products.

Many people feel much better whenever they wash their hair and believe this is just because their hair is physically cleaner. This is partially true but the main reason is because the process of washing often clears two energy blockages, Soul 5 and Cosmic 5, and they feel better because their energy and cleansing functions are stepped up. The blockages appear because of a weakness of the protection of Spirit. People who feel they must wash their hair very frequently would be well advised to take one feverfew tablet daily.

The two following anecdotes are indicative of the importance of hair and skin for well-being. About sixteen years ago I was suffering from dandruff. I bought a remedy and rubbed some into my scalp with the result that the dandruff was cleared within days. With the benefit of hindsight I can now see that the remedy cleared an energy blockage from my scalp, Earth 3, but blocked another energy, Mind 3. The release of the Earth energy improved my proximity healing whereas the Mind blockage impaired the clearance of toxins from my blood. However both were needed to assist in a major change in my urinary system leading to a vastly improved cleansing function which is now working. The other anecdote also relates to hair. Over the past few months each time I applied vaseline hair tonic to my hair an energy, Air 3, was unblocked, but now that my respiration system is being controlled by the correct part of the brain those blockages have ceased.

It can be seen from the above that metabolism is a function of the whole being and that attempts to improve it by conventional measures will usually be unsuccessful. In this system of healing at some stage hand healing will usually be needed.

Nutritional Supplements and Remedies

There is a huge range of safe and effective remedies available from health food shops. They have the advantage over most modern drugs in that they are cheap and if necessary can be taken for long periods without any adverse side-effects. Most of the remedies mentioned in this section are recommended by the manufacturers for treating specific adverse conditions. For example each Bach remedy is recommended for the correction of a specific adverse emotional or psychological condition, and most herbal remedies are directed at alleviating coughs, colds, headaches and the like. The use of the pendulum however enables the right remedy to be discovered for any function, thus taking into account the non-physical and subtle elements of the Being. Keen and expert healers may wish to have at their disposal a much bigger range of remedies, but most will find that those mentioned are adequate because many healers, and their patients, will receive help from the holistic healing network which is now in being. This network is available because of the disappearance of a miasm, Universe 10, which had blocked the distribution of a vital healing energy, Soul 7, since the Biblical fall.

If anyone is ill he needs the best nutrition possible. Much can be done by dowsing the best food and beverages, but sometimes the patient's digestion may be very much impaired in which case nutritional supplements may be necessary. This also applies to many people who have a chronically poor digestion. The following food supplements will often be helpful:

Lecithin, Brewers Yeast, Wheat Germ Oil, Kelp & Spirulina.

There are a number of problems which involve all the

functions when energies are blocked outside the skin or in the body tissues. The principal causes are black magic, witchcraft and bad influences, which are the main reasons for depression, neurosis and the like. In such cases the following could be helpful:

Garlic Perles, Honey, Lecithin, Brewers Yeast, Juna Beans, Oil of Olbas and the Bach Rescue Remedy.

The latter two may be applied to the indicated part of the skin or taken orally.

Herbal remedies can cleanse the body tissues of poisons, toxins and disease residues which are blocking the main environmental energies and thus reducing vitality. The following are useful for this purpose:

Ginseng tablets, Black Willow Compound tablets, Saffron Seed Oil capsules, Gravel Root Compound tablets, Cranesbill Compound tablets, Cider Vinegar capsules, Echinacea tablets, Garlic Perles and Rose Hip tablets.

Subtle energies can become blocked when levels of consciousness are blocked due to an underactive pancreas in the energy function. This is a very common condition which affects most people beyond the age of fifty. All the functions are affected. Another big problem is when glandular secretions begin to fail. Right vitamins can be helpful for both these conditions as there is a vitamin corresponding to every gland. In most people the pituitary gland fails at an early age but fortunately a well balanced diet, including fruit, vegetables and wholemeal grain, largely makes good the deficiency. Most elderly people would feel much better if they were to take some vitamin E on a regular basis. For any condition of illness or poor health it is essential to examine the need for vitamins. In diseases where protection fails, such as AIDS, a massive intake of vitamin B6 is necessary. Biotin can be very helpful when virility is low due to underactive sex glands. No more vitamins should be taken than is necessary because, if too many are taken over a long period, for some people the action of the liver in the Energising function can be depressed. For prolonged use Rose Hip tablets will always be helpful.

In addition to the remedies mentioned above the following may be helpful for the functions:

Function 1	Energy	The appropriate Tissue Salt
Function 2	Sensory	Oil of Sandalwood inhaled as necessary
Function 3	Elimination	Kelp tablets
Function 4	Muscular	Pulsatilla Compound tablets
Function 5	Sexual	Garlic Perles
Function 6	Thinking	Rutin Compound tablets
Function 7	Healing	The Bach Rescue Remedy
Function 8	Cleansing	Vita Florem
Function 9	Control	Pakua
Function 10	Protection	Feverfew tablets

Beginners may from time to time like to check the efficacy of the remedies they prescribe by using the model to find out what beneficial effects have followed after a remedy has been taken. The following examples are typical.

An old dog, Jill. Protection against psychic agression poor. Reason, Cosmic Chakra 9 was blocked. Had been in distress for some time because of black magic attacks. She was a target because of her great healing power. Her speciality, the Soul. The attack opened up her Soul Chakra 6 to a Cosmic energy. Feverfew tablets opened up her Cosmic Chakra 9 with lasting benefit.

Myself. Whilst typing, a problem I sometimes encounter is the blocking of Mind, level of consciousness 6, because I am unconsciously giving distant healing to people with Mind problems and taking blockages off them. When Mind level of consciousness 6 is blocked I am unable to scan the information files I need for intuitive typing. One Calcium Sulphate tissue salt tablet clears the blockage immediately. This is a problem many people encounter in their daily life.

An elderly man came to me because of neck and shoulder pains but he had much deeper problems than that. I treated him on the basis of 'what shall I do now?' and at one stage I dabbed a little Oil of Olbas on the back of his hand. This opened up Sun Chakra 4 which had been blocked for ten years and had caused extreme muscular tension. At the end of a lengthy session the pain had gone and the hypertension was clearing.

Foods and Drugs – Dependencies and Addictions

As already mentioned many animals and some humans can live on a very simple diet; they do not need a wide range of foods to be healthy and vigorous. This is because animals and some humans living a simpler life than we do have powerful cleansing functions which enable them to cleanse their immediate environment so that they can receive the subtle energies they need. All they require in addition is the food to provide calorific energy. The necessary proteins are produced by the metabolism. A long time ago man had this gift of cleansing but this was lost when he became opened up to a new level of consciousness 1, (obligations). This permitted one new energy and its associated level of consciousness, Mind 6, (perceptions) to enter. Man became *homo sapiens*. He became self conscious. This caused a new disease unique to mankind, disseminated sclerosis, and resulted in a major constitutional change. The digestive and defecation systems were drastically changed so that people were unable to generate some of the energies needed for cleansing their environment and a varied diet became essential. That is why most of us are dependent on a fairly wide range of foods if we are to have the higher functions of imagination, healing, cleansing, energising and protection. Man had to pay a high price for his self consciousness. He acquired a conscience and became a feeble, sickly creature. People with the superior constitution I have described will be able to live on almost anything. It has taken us a long time to regain something we lost at the price of a conscience.

Some people are further dependent on alcohol, tobacco and drugs such as cannabis and cocaine. All can become addictions. We take alcohol for two main reasons, for social occasions and for protection. Most of us at a party or when entertaining friends feel the need for some alcohol to break down some of the inhibitions imposed on us by our obligations. We feel happier because we are able to meet people at Soul level which we may not otherwise be able to do. Some people are allergic to alcohol and are thus unable to get the benefits it can bring and some people never need it because their level of consciousness 10 (future) is subconsciously working, thus relieving them of the feelings of anxiety to which many of us are subject. Some people need alcohol, particularly of an evening, to gain protective energies which their metabolism is unable to provide. These are Mind, Soul, Spirit, Cosmic and Universe 10. These people are sensitives whose perception 8 (spirits) has been opened without the necessary protection. They are also vulnerable to psychic aggression and bad influences. If they do not take alcohol they are likely to be in constant need of Valium or some similar drug. They then lose in some degree their intuition, healing, cleansing and protection. Alcohol, as Sir Winston Churchill would have testified, does not have these side-effects. He was no cabbage! I have found it necessary to take a whisky at bedtime for the past thirty years for the provision of protective energies, and since my attack of AIDS in recent years I have found it necessary to take a gin and mixed vermouth before supper. This has given me pretty good protection against psychic aggression and bad influences.

Many people need to smoke because they are deficient in Nature energies as a result of a constitutional weakness in the elimination function which results in poor cleansing of toxins from the blood. If they do not smoke their thinking, healing and cleansing functions are impaired. However, many smokers are unwittingly taking toxins from other people by distant healing. I can speak on this from experience. I have been a heavy smoker for many years and since

AIDS a very heavy smoker, because all my life I have been taking toxins from people and since I began to heal I have been taking toxins from all my patients. Nicotine has also been necessary to clear poison from my system. Since I have been very sensitive my guru, Sai Baba, has repeatedly told me that I must smoke until I acquire my improved constitution.

An addiction is formed when the spirit, the essence, of a food, beverage or drug finds its way into Soul level of consciousness 2 (needs). It is possession. This occurs because the kidneys are unable effectively to clear the discarnates which occupy it from the blood, which happens when the urinary system is controlled by the part of the brain which should be controlling lymph circulation. It usually takes time for alcohol, tobacco and cannabis to become addictions, but the hard drugs can cause immediate addiction because they block levels of consciousness 9 and 10 (right path and future) with the result that the victim loses most of his guidance and is unable to foresee the future unconsciously. He feels lost and isolated and is in a state of great anxiety until he can get the next fix. Also, with hard drugs the conscience is blocked.

People take the hard drugs because it makes them feel good. These all in some measure knock out level of consciousness 1 (obligations). They are thus relieved of subconscious worries about things they should have done and have not done. Conscience, the basis of our humanity, disappears. Many people taking hallucinatory drugs open up very high levels of consciousness for which they are not ready and for which they may never be ready in their lifetime. They are entering Ouspensky's noumenal world, a world in which they have no place.

The only proper way of treating addiction is by healing and by paying careful attention to diet and nutritional supplements because all addicts are undernourished. For successful healing the healer will need to have Universe consciousness in order to heal the Air Body which is the body most affected. At present the number of healers with Universe Consciousness is very small but the number will increase rapidly over the next twelve months. In addition to the 'what shall I do now?' healing, the Metamorphic Technique which is described in a later section will be very beneficial. This technique would be very good for hostels or hospitals where addicts are being treated because the patients, after a little instruction, could treat each other. In addition to dowsing a tailor-made diet the following nutritional supplements will be needed – honey, lecithin and brewers yeast – and to clear the body tissues of drug residues and toxins some or all of the following will be needed – ginseng, echinacea tablets, garlic perles and rose hip tablets. Attempts to clear addictions by conventional methods are a waste of time when it is the Soul which is screaming for help.

Allergies

An allergy manifests when a subtle energy, either from an external field or from a food, beverage or drug, finds its way into the wrong functional control channel causing a bizarre response. The sources can be food, beverages, humans and animals, objects which are touched or radiations from naturally occurring or synthetic substances. The effects of allergies are various. There may be pain, nausea, migraine and bad skin and hair conditions; and often there may be problems not generally regarded as being caused by allergies, such as rheumatism, arthritis and mental and emotional disorders. One of the many sources rarely recognised is limestone and the lime contained in mortar and concrete.

All allergies result in a weakening of protection thus leaving the subject open to many ailments. Medical tests can only bring to light a very small proportion of the sources of allergies: dowsing can reveal many more but at present few dowsers can detect many of the allergies involving the Sun, Nature, Air, Water, Spirit, Cosmic and Universe Bodies. To detect an allergy a dowser needs to be able to perceive the offending energy. To detect all possible allergies, which number 110, the dowser would need consciousness of all the bodies and chakras. No allergies can be detected with the pendulum unless the dowser's Air Body, level of consciousness 6 and levels of perception 1, 2 and 3 are working fully. Healers' perception of allergies will improve as they work on holistic lines. Blocking the offending energies is of course very beneficial but unless the root systemic problem is corrected the patient will continue to be deprived of one or more beneficial energies. The principal weaknesses are in the Air Body and the sensory and control functions. The organ usually involved is the pancreas. By touch healing of the hands and face allergies can be blocked and necessary systemic changes set in train. It may be many months before these become effective thus enabling the patient to receive the beneficial energies of which he was deprived.

If good allergies are identified and the healer is unable to block them the patient can steer clear of the offending food, but it is not possible to keep away from allergy sources such as silica (earth), subsoils, plastics and many others. In such cases if the healer cannot block the harmful energies he may be able to prescribe a course of tissue salts, either singly or in combination, which will alleviate the patient's condition. Feverfew tablets are helpful for all allergic conditions.

Allergies are always present in any illness or adverse mental or emotional condition. The following are the principal offending energies and foods for some chronic illnesses.

Cancer	Universe 10	Any sort of grain
Rheumatism	Cosmic 10	Meat
Arthritis	Spirit 10	Potatoes
Stroke	Soul 10	Sugar
Insanity	Mind 10	Cheese
Impotence	Nature 10	Butter
Migraine	Sun 10	Cows milk
Depression	Water 10	Citrus fruits
Irrational Behaviour	Air 10	Legumes
Insomnia	Earth 10	Coffee

The new and much publicised illness AIDS is one of the new diseases that have appeared in recent years as new environmental energies become available. There are more to come within the next year or two. In addition to many of the types of allergy mentioned above all AIDS sufferers have one thing in common, an allergy to all humans and animals, ie. to blood.

Some healers, such as Clive Harris and John Cain, are able to clear many allergies by touch or hand healing. This is because they have a digestion which can generate Universe 7, an energy which at present is rarely available as an environmental energy. It is however becoming more readily available and more healers will get this necessary power in the near future.

Our Interdependence with Other People and Other Forms of Life

In the six years since the big change in the state of my non-physical and physical constitution began, our inter-dependence with other forms of life has been demonstrated to me daily in my healing work. It has been proved to me beyond any shadow of doubt that no healing can be holistic unless this relationship with other forms of life is recognised and becomes a major aspect of healing. Looking back this seems so obvious, but only seven years ago I had little inkling of it. As my Universe Consciousness opened so I saw more clearly this life relationship, and it is clear that the paramount need in the world today is the rapid spread of holistic healing so that Universe Consciousness becomes commonplace throughout the world. It is only when this state is achieved, or well on the way to attainment, that man will be more able to discharge his responsibilities for the Earth and the animal and nature kingdoms.

As is to be expected, our main responsibilities are towards our fellows. In this and other lives we have interacted – that is there have been exchanges of etheric elements – with people we have met, particularly with those with whom we have been emotionally involved; and also with some we may never have met. Although some of these exchanges, when recognised, may have seemed to be unpleasant, diminishing and random, it is not so. In the long term they are all purposeful and sooner or later, in this life or in others, result in expanded awareness and a superior constitution. When a healer has Universe Consciousness he is able, without conscious effort, to reverse these exchanges in his normal distant or hand healing routines. When this happens it marks the end of a period of learning. In my experience the most common lesson that most people are now learning is knowledge and understanding of the nature kingdom and of the Earth. When working alone, almost every day I have been guided to think of people I have met in the past, sometimes childhood friends, with whom I have interacted. I know that I have had about a hundred significant interactions with other people in my life, starting with my wet-nurse, and the two biggest lessons I have learned from all these encounters are knowledge and understanding of the nature kingdom and the Earth.

Animals, particularly our pets, are much involved in this interactive process and some are also very much involved in the healing process. Our aged labrador Jill became heavily involved in healing about five years ago when she got Universe Consciousness, and now she is a very good healer of men and women, some of whom she thinks about a great deal. She is particularly good on healing Soul. She does not think much about other dogs. This is not surprising as dogs do not know envy as we do. Two or three years ago I met a woman who had a cottage in Wales. She said it was very 'dirty' and asked if I could clean it up. I told her that I was not able to but that I knew someone who could. After a moment or two I saw that it was a job for Jill, and there and then I put her in mental touch with the cottage. A year later I saw the woman again; she was profuse in her thanks and said the cottage felt lovely. It had taken Jill seven hours to clear away witchcraft residues from the cottage. After that she had given healing to the woman's son. I now know that Jill blocked a harmful energy from the man by giving up one of her own energy inputs, but that she got it back.

My most dramatic experience with animals concerns one
of those most beautiful creatures, a killer whale. I saw a
programme on TV about a Dutch zoologist who wanted a
killer whale to research the possibility of communicating
with it. When a young whale was fished up off the New-
foundland coast the zoologist was amazed because once
they got her on deck she showed no signs of fear; her pulse
and respiration were normal. In Holland she was put in a
dolphinarium, separated from the dolphins. Although she
could not see them, as soon as they began their performance
she went through the same routine as they did. After a time
the zoologist found that he could communicate with her in
three ways. When asked to come and take something from
him she would do so, but one day she swam to him with
something in her mouth and said "You take it." It was then
that I realised that it was not the professor who was in
charge, it was Gudron, the whale. The next day I was able
to get in touch with Gudron and have worked with her
many times, since when she has given healing to me and to
many of my healer friends and patients. Like the dolphins
she has, so far as I can judge, a near perfect non-physical and
physical constitution. Her main healing task is to help the
healing of man's Sun Body which is largely concerned with
human happiness, muscular activity and coordination. In
1981 I visited the Golden Rock temple at Trichinopoly in
India where an elephant receives the visitors at the entrance.
She takes their contributions which she acknowledges by a
gentle tap on the head with her trunk. She had been helping
me for three years before I saw her. The main help she gave,
and is giving to me, is in healing Spirit.

Two or three years ago a young woman phoned me to
ask if I could help her horse which had been 'down' for
several days. Over the phone I told her that she herself was
the main problem and before going to see the horse I gave
her some healing to clear her emotional trouble. At the
stable I showed her where to place her hands for a few

minutes on the horse. I then touched it on the head whereupon it got to its feet and let rip an enormous fart to the
delight of a small group of onlookers.

After the big change, my involvement with plants was
soon demonstrated when I found that what few gardening
gifts I possessed had disappeared. Neither flowers nor vegetables flourished; in fact many plants would not grow at all.
It was the same story with indoor plants; nothing would
grow. We were given a beautiful indoor weeping fuchsia
which died in a few days. I knew of course that this gardening catastrophe was connected with my healing work, but it
is only now that I can 'see' what it was all about. In this new
phase, the role of all the plants was to give protection to
healing friends and patients until such time as systemic
changes had been initiated. A remarkable event happened at
Christmas in 1983. I was showing a friend how to 'feel' the
life force on an indoor azalea when she began to give it hand
healing. This went on for about ten minutes, none of us
knowing what was happening. Next day I found out that
she had been giving healing through the plant to the Cosmic
Body of a Swedish woman, the friend of a friend of mine.
None of us had met her. Next day the plant looked very sick
and I discovered it was busy healing the Nature Bodies of
some of my friends. The next time I enquired about its
activities I found it was healing a small unhappy hydrangea
in the back garden.

As might be expected, trees figure prominently in holistic
healing. A few minutes' walk from our bungalow are some
splendid oak-trees, about three hundred years old. One in
particular is a friend I have to visit and touch. Its particular
job for me was to give protection while my Nature Body
was renewed and brought into service. It also has a com-
munication role. Whilst in India I knew there was a tree I
had to visit and touch. This turned out to be at a ruined city
near Bijapur and I had no difficulty in finding it. When I
touched the tree it sent 'knowledge' of the Universe Body

to my oak-tree friend who passed it on to my wife who in turn passed it on to a woman friend who needed it. My oak-tree is also in touch with some woodland in Pennsylvania. I have not enquired what it is up to.

In our sub-levels of consciousness 4 (fellow-workers) should be humans, animals and spirit representatives of the earth, plants and trees. This should not surprise us. Cleve Backster and Dr Marcel Vogel, Chief Scientist to IBM and one of the world's greatest physicists, have proved under laboratory conditions that plants can receive our thoughts. The elephant, the killer whale and other animals are amongst my fellow-workers.

Psychic Aggression

This is a subject of tremendous importance to society but regrettably the medical profession and the establishment generally pretend that it does not exist. This is because, whilst we pay lip-service to such concepts as Soul, Mind and Spirit, in practice medical practitioners treat us as if we were machines. Many people – spiritualists, healers and aggressors – are involved in it but the vast majority of the general public are in total ignorance of the subject which has a profound bearing on our health and happiness. It is achieved by projecting, by thought, chakras or bodies of humans or animals (living or discarnate) at the tissues or skin of people. When around the skin, environmental energies are blocked and, when directed at body tissues, vitalities are blocked. While most of this aggression is achieved by conscious thought there are some people, like some healers, who do their work unconsciously.

It is to be expected that the Church would be expert in these matters, bearing in mind the responsibility it claims for the non-physical aspects of man, its long history and the vast number of esoteric books and documents in its possession, but if this is so the Church seems to keep it very much to itself. Although a few parsons do healing in their churches and I believe they occasionally hold services to clear people of what they term 'possession', one must assume that the bulk of the work of their many sensitives is done remotely. Do they try to heal the non-physical bodies of members of the public generally or do they reserve their attentions for church-goers only? In my experience it seems that their main concern is to limit rather than widen the awareness of their parishioners by attacking sensitives outside the church.

I recently read a good book, *Healing the Family Tree*, by Dr Kenneth McCall, which dealt with possession and exorcism. He gave many examples of people being healed of 'possession' during special church services. There is no doubt he has great healing gifts and that he was the main channel of healing wherever the service was held and whoever presided over it. Whilst in no way wishing to belittle the work he has done, we must not exclude people of other religious beliefs, nor agnostics or atheists. Holistic healing is not the property of any specific religion.

Paracelsus had strong words to say about the role of the church in healing possession in his day. It still seems to be true.

"Some people believe that such spirits can be driven away with holy water and by the burning of incense, but a genuine holy water cannot be had so long as no man is found who is holy enough to be able to invest water with an occult power and the odour of incense may sooner attract evil spirits than drive them away because evil spirits are attracted by things that are attractive to the senses, and if we wish to drive them away it would be more reasonable to employ disagreeable odours for such a purpose. The true and effective power against all evil spirits is the will; if we love the source of all good with all our heart, mind and desire, we may be sure never to fall into the power of evil; but priestly ceremonies – the sprinkling of water, the burning of incense, and the singing of incantations – are the inventions of clerical vanity, and they therefore take their origin from the source of all evil. Ceremonies have been instituted originally to give an external form to an internal act but, where the internal power to perform such acts does not exist, a ceremony will be of no avail except to attract such spirits as may love to mock at our foolishness."

Psychic aggression has been prevalent in most countries for many thousands of years, but the past forty years have seen a tremendous increase in its use. Many individuals direct their aggression at others for reasons of hatred, envy or jealousy, but much is highly organised and used by skilled operators. On the TV recently an author was being interviewed about a book he had written on the subject of freemasonry. In the discussion he said that the movement had been penetrated by the KGB. I have no doubt that he was correct because I already believed that many governments use these methods. I further believe that most of our institutions, many businesses and trade unions, religious and pseudo-religious movements and societies of many kinds are also using or are subverted by these methods or both. Some are in it for money, some because they want to destroy a society they hate and some, for the best of intentions, want to impose on society what they think is best for us.

It is remarkable that, with so many clerics and presumably a good many doctors being aware of the prevalence of psychic aggression, so few of these custodians of our spiritual and physical health so far have had the guts to bring the subject into the open. So we have a situation where tens of thousands of people with ailments having non-physical causes are committed to a permanent regime of highly complex chemicals for the rest of their lives, treated with drugs which restrict the awareness and impair their non-physical functioning. It is worth remembering that the main income of the drug companies comes from patients on a long term or permanent regime of drugs. It is therefore to be expected that they would bitterly oppose any organised move on the part of the medical profession to use healers to provide a back-up service. But individual doctors could make a start by keeping their eyes open for healers and giving them a chance. At the worst they would give some comfort and at the best the patients would be cured and healed. In his book, *Paradise Gained*, Dr Arthur Guirdham, the distinguished psychiatrist, attributes migraine, Menières syndrome, accident proneness, severe allergies and cancer to psychic aggression. I am sure he could have named many more. Incidentally, in the book he gives the church a real lambasting but I cannot recall any criticism of the medical profession or his fellow psychiatrists. I hope he has not totally failed to convince some of his fellow medics of the reality of psychic aggression.

Until about three years ago I considered these activities to be fundamentally evil; in other words I was a dualist believing in fundamental good and evil, but when I attained Spirit Consciousness I realised that these activities were no more random and fortuitous than the vast healing movement presently under way. Like everything else, if we could but see it, they are under Divine Guidance. The aggressors' job is to waken us up, to open up our consciousness and perceptions, many of which have been blocked for a very long time. No aggression is admitted except with the consent of our Spirit which will accept the right aggression and exclude that which we do not need. Many healers take elaborate precautions to protect themselves but in the long run this may not be a good thing because they may be preventing their awareness from expanding as it needs to do. There is another way of dealing with these problems which some healers will be able to use. If you can perceive that you are under attack and you can perceive which element of your being is under attack, find out what the problem is and clear it. It may be a disease miasm from this or another life or a character block from this or another life. A common target is Soul sub-level 7 which should be possessed by love but is instead possessed by fear. The major objective of all this is that we should be opened up to Cosmic, ie. Christ Consciousness. Some of the many gifts which come with that are tolerance, reason and protection.

Psychic aggression should not be regarded as a special thing needing particular attention. It is just one of those problems which healers encounter in their work. At the right time aggressors will be healed and they are no more to be judged than healers are to be commended. It is something that will increasingly be handled by the thousands of healers in this country working quietly on their own.

Ageing and Constitutional Change

The ageing problem begins at birth when Cosmic Chakra 8 is blocked to preserve life. This impairs the operation of the lymph system in the elimination function. There are a few people who are fortunate and do not have a karmic blockage dating back to the time when the earth's magnetic field strength increased sharply over the course of a few months. What these lucky people possess is a lymph system which circulates and effectively cleanses the body tissues. The pump which effects the circulation is the prostate gland, an organ which for most of us is just a nuisance. These people with a good lymph system have effective cleansing of the lymph by the gall-bladder. The result is superior blood and greater vitality. Also, their blood receives throughout life the thymus secretion, which in most of us begins to dry up at an early age.

Another cause of premature ageing is weakness of functioning of the endocrine system. Again this goes back to birth when Nature Chakra 5, which is necessary for good metabolism, is blocked. This causes a reduction in Spirit Chakra 6 which weakens mental and healing powers, and the feeling of general well-being. Dowsers will be able to 'see' that the blockage was needed to preserve life after the main Air field strength increased and man's constitution was unable to handle it.

Yet another reason for premature ageing concerns the pituitary gland. Up to puberty one role is to promote

physical growth and afterwards it should produce a secretion to protect the body from infectious disease. In fact in
most of us the gland ceases to function. External protection
is provided but at the cost of several cosmic energies which
cannot penetrate the special protection. If that special protection is lost serious illnesses such as pneumonia, influenza
and many others can occur. The karmic cause of this problem was a big increase in Nature energies.

With holistic healing the above defects can be eliminated
and many constitutional changes can be set in train resulting
in new or improved systems. Moreover there is an increase in
the inter-connection of the systems so that when necessary it
is easier for healthy systems to help defective ones. One task
of the systems is to generate vitalities from the environment
fields, which are needed for proper functioning. Substitute
energies can be generated by the complete digestion of the
right foods, but it is rare for the shortfall to be fully made up
in this way. As most of us are constituted at present two
energies cannot be received in the right systems; they are Sun
and Universe. To receive them properly the lymph and
circulation systems have to be radically changed. As some of
these Sun and Universe energies are essential for life they
have to be generated in part by the genital and respiration
systems. This results in impairment of the sexual, cleansing
and elimination functions. Two other energies usually in
short supply are Water and Mind. This can be rectified when,
for the purpose of generation of subtle energies, the digestive
system as we generally understand it is split into digestion
and defecation. The major systemic changes are as follows:

1 A mass of new ducts is built so that the lymph system
   becomes a closed circulating system with the prostate
   gland serving as the pump. Cleansing of the lymph is
   effected by a modified gall-bladder.
2 The appendix ceases to be an appendix and becomes
   the stub of a new duct from the gall-bladder. This
   provides superior cleansing of the bowel.

3 Digestive processes are changed so that almost all of them take place within the stomach. The small intestine is shortened.
4 New ducts are provided from the spleen to the pylorus and from the pancreas to the duodenum to give better digestion.
5 In addition to its role in the lymph system the prostate gland also has a role in the sexual function.

Many illnesses occur when systems are trying to change to a superior arrangement. Holistic healing can facilitate these changes. To be able to do so the healer's Soul Chakra 10 and Universe Chakra 7 have to be fully working.

Analysis of Some Dis-eases

It is possible for a dowser with Universe Consciousness to analyse the course of dis-ease and to check the beneficial or adverse effects of foods, remedies and drugs. The following brief examples demonstrate the value of the model.

Chicken Pox. This occurs when energy Nature 5 finds its way into the wrong channel, Cosmic 5. If the disease were allowed to run its course, very speedily Energy Mind 6 would be blocked and the acute problem would cease. The end result is that the pancreas is damaged and the protection, sexual and elimination functions are impaired. The principal allergy manifesting in the acute stage is to flour.

Measles. This is caused by Nature 1 getting into the channel for Cosmic 1. To preserve life, Soul 4 is blocked. Continuing after-effects, until the gall-bladder is repaired by healing, are a reduction in physical energy, while the elimination of toxins from the blood and cleansing of the body tissues are also impaired. The principal allergy in the acute stage is to eggs.

Scarlet Fever. This occurs when Soul 1 gets into the Nature 1 channel. The organ to suffer most is the spleen. The continuing effect is poor protection against energy fields and spirits. The principal allergy is to butter.

Rheumatism. This is caused by the blockage of energy Water 9. The result is inferior lymph which is unable effectively to clear toxins from the muscles. Two organs suffer, the heart and the liver. Correction can be a long job because brain repairs are needed to make good the lymph and para-sympathetic nervous systems. Five allergic conditions are present, to silica (earth), clay, limestone, magma and sand.

Bad Circulation. This again is caused by a blocked chakra, Soul 9. It happens when the protection of the Earth Body is poor and an unsuitable Universe spirit is picked up. Likely places for this to happen are Universe energy sites. The brain blockage can be cleared by healing. The principal allergy which appears is to water.

Depression. Attacks occur when level of consciousness 8 is blocked and support of 'brothers and sisters' with emotional problems is not forthcoming. The root problem is poor protection of the pancreas in the Spirit. The principal allergy is to coffee.

Osteo-Arthritis. This is caused by two blocked chakras, Earth 9 and Mind 4. The initial weaknesses are in the spleen and pancreas in the Cosmic Body. To effect a cure, it is necessary to repair these two organs. The blockages are often picked up at a Water Centre. The principal allergy is to meat.

Irrational Behaviour. This happens when sub-levels of consciousness of Mind are blocked. Most commonly these are levels 1 and 2 when the sufferer becomes confused about obligations and needs. The principal allergy is to sugar.

Stress. The worst result of stress is unhappiness. It is caused by frustration which depresses the function of the liver in the Sun Body and impairs cleansing of the flesh tissue which then blocks in some degree the ingress of Earth energies. The principal allergy is to fruit.

Migraine. This is caused by Sun energy 4 getting into channel Soul 4. The basic weakness is the heart in the Water Body. Feverfew blocks the offending energy. The principal allergy is to tea.

AIDS. This is one of the new diseases caused by Universe 4 which for the past few years has become more generally available, as a miasm caused by rheumatism is being cleared. It occurs when the energy gets into Cosmic 9 with the result that there is almost total failure of the protection. Dozens of allergies appear but the principal one is to blood.

Legionnaires Disease. This is another new disease caused by Universe 10 getting into channel Air 2. This causes total failure of the protection against bad influences.

Disseminated Sclerosis. This is caused by Spirit 8 getting into Earth 8. The root problem is failure of many non–physical channels (nerve substitutes) due to shock or psychic aggression. The primary problem is caused by lack of energy Soul 3. Three organs are badly damaged, the spleen, gall-bladder and pancreas. The three nervous systems are also damaged in the brain. Many allergies result, the principal one being to dairy products.

Water Retention. This is a very common complaint particularly amongst older people. It is usually caused by black magic but it can occur naturally. Water retention occurs when the drainage ducts from the body cavities are blocked. The most serious condition is when the lungs become water-logged and the heart is overstressed in trying to secure sufficient oxygen for the blood. The operator blocks off environmental Soul energies by projecting a chakra or chakras into the flesh of the victim, causing partial failure of the elimination function. Sufferers are vulnerable because of the failure of the pancreas in level 10 of the Cosmic Body. This is often brought about by poisoning by a molybdenum salt. A course of feverfew tablets will clear the poison. First-aid treatment in the event of an attack is the Bach Rescue remedy. I am able to write on this subject from personal experience having been given the poison in beer and later subjected to an attack which was successful.

Thrombosis. Seven times out of ten this is caused by black magic. The operator projects a chakra at the epidermis of the victim thus blocking off environmental Cosmic energies. This causes overloading of the Sun Body which causes the protection of the Spirit to fail leading to the blockage of blood vessels. The psychic attack is usually preceded by aluminium poisoning. I have withstood several such attacks because having a good digestion I was able to extract the necessary Sun energies from my food. The aluminium can be cleared by feverfew tablets.

High Blood Pressure. This is another chronic complaint in the same category as the two preceding cases. By black magic some muscles are blocked to Sun energies with adverse effects on the cardio-vascular system. The poison used is aluminium.

Chronic disease can occur as a result of imbalances in any of the subtle bodies but most originate in the Cosmic Body. They usually begin when many non-physical channels fail as a result of exposure to miasms, bad influences or physical or mental shock. This causes a drop in control energy for proper functioning. Metabolism, elimination and non-physical cleansing suffer most. The reduction in non-physical cleansing results in a bad influence around the body which cuts out the main Spirit field and further reduces protection against bad influences. The net result is that the blood is not properly cleansed. Rheumatism, arthritis and other degenerative diseases may ensue. Dowsers will be able to find from the model the train of events for other diseases as they require in the course of their work.

It is stressed that the above analyses are given to demonstrate the power of this system of healing and the value of this approach to the medical profession and to the manufacturers of drugs. It could be unwise for any but the most experienced healers to set out to cure any acute or chronic conditions resulting from any clinical diagnosis. A host of other problems may be present which may prevent successful healing. The best approach for any healer is to ignore diagnoses or symptoms and start from a position of total ignorance and work on the basis of 'what shall I do now?' because almost invariably the root problem is remote from the symptom.

Some Reasons for Illness and Unhappiness

Everyone at birth has an allotted life span. If this is not fulfilled the Soul becomes earthbound until it is healed or until the allotted span is reached. The most common reason for becoming ill and unhappy or dying an untimely death is exposure to harmful radiations. These may emanate from energy centres, from many industrial processes, from x-ray equipment and of recent years from microwave ovens. These radiations damage one or more of the auras and leave the subject exposed to invasion by spirits. They may be from anything; from humans, animals, plants and objects. This blocks chakras and prevents the generation of vitalities whether they are derived from food or from the environment. If sufficient chakras are blocked this can lead to illness or unhappiness. This aggression is permitted by the Spirit in an attempt to open up level 7 of the Soul to love. Healers with Soul Consciousness can open this with the result that the 'aggression' ceases.

Another prime source of illness is an inferior constitution. The weaknesses can be of many types but most commonly at fault are the urinary and lymph systems. The most common problem with the urinary system is its failure adequately to cleanse toxins from the blood. Most lymph systems do not adequately cleanse the brain and body tissues with the result that they become silted up, vitalities are reduced and diseases such as senile decay, arthritis, rheumatism and nephritis result. Another serious weakness is a poor digestion which cannot generate the vitalities needed for good health. Such constitutional weaknesses can only be cleared by a healer with Universe Consciousness. Usually cure will be a lengthy process because work has to be done on brain, systems and tissues.

People can be born selfish, greedy and hypocritical and sail moronically through life, being happy and healthy in their state of restricted awareness, but if new perceptions and levels of consciousness open up they may find they have problems. The opening up of these levels is not the result of conscious effort on the part of these people. It can happen as a result of meeting a particular person, as a result of psychic aggression or an accident or merely by visiting some locality and being exposed to a new energy. The ones who are likely to sail through life without many bumps are those who live a quiet domestic and conventional life. Many things can happen as a result of being opened up; the most common being physical illness such as rheumatism, arthritis and cancer. These come about when a level, which may have been blocked for a long time is opened up and the disease miasm is exposed. Other undesirable effects are depression, fear and unhappiness. These can occur when levels of consciousness are opened up which have been blocked to conceal something of which the person is ashamed or afraid. A common cause of trouble is when some mean or despicable act one has committed is subconsciously recalled. Thus in this life we may suffer for past actions. We can also be tormented by remembering bad things we have done in this life. The memories which trouble us most are instances of cruelty or cowardice. Adverse conditions to do ith unpleasant memories, perceptions and levels of consciousness can be cleared by a healer with Cosmic Consciousness.

Until the past forty years or so poisoning was a rare occurrence and usually took place against a domestic background. In recent years there has been a vast increase in the incidence of poisoning mainly by the use of poisons in homeopathic potencies which cannot be detected by conventional analysis. Most of the poisoners are professionals who have been 'spotted' and recruited by some organisation with aggressive intentions. The main object of the poisoning is to impair the target's protection so that his mind can be controlled or his reason blocked by distant action. Also of course the poor protection leaves the target open to a vast variety of illnesses. The targets are invariably sensitives who unconsciously open up the awareness of other people. This is counter to the aspirations of the aggressors whose intention is to limit the awareness of the public so that they become more amenable to direction. So, many of the organisations who are continually bleating about democracy are in fact subversively trying to bring about a state of enslavement. A vast range of poisons are currently in use, two popular ones being aluminium and novocaine. Doctors, unless they are good dowsers cannot detect these instances of poisoning. They can all be cleared by healers with Sun Consciousness. If such a healer is unavailable much can be done with herbs and tissue salts.

Bereavement is a very common cause of illness. Extreme reactions occur where the lost partner has been giving much protection to the other and where the survivor's Spirit level 7, love, is blocked. Sufferers can be healed by healers with Spirit Consciousness. Much can be done by the extended use of Bach remedies.

Finally of course another common source of illness and unhappiness is accidents. Some people are accident prone, not only do they have accidents but things often go wrong in their domestic and business lives. Their problem lies in the mind. This is when their mind is unable to perceive the right message from the Spirit which has already accepted the right plans. Accident proneness can be cleared by healers with Mind Consciousness.

The Healing Process

The term complementary medicine covers all schools and types of healing which are outside conventional medicine, such as chiropractic, osteopathy, acupuncture, homoeopathy etc. and the healing which is the subject of this book. Some of the formal disciplines such as chiropractic and osteopathy may appear to rely mainly on physical skills of manipulation, but in fact every successful practitioner has gifts of proximity and touch healing: similarly every good orthodox doctor has these gifts to some degree. Most of these therapies are fairly specialised in that, usually, each is successful in treating specific elements of the Being. For example hypnotherapy is very good for healing Mind which is our biggest problem, chiropractic is good for clearing traumas which block the Cosmic Body and impair functioning, and acupuncture is good for healing the Nature Body. Apart from the remedies and drugs they dispense General Practitioners are good at healing the Soul by proximity and touch. Some of them would do much better if they were to shake hands with their patients. Only one type of healing – holistic healing – can heal the perceptions and levels of consciousness and put in hand systemic change leading to superior constitutions. The effectiveness of holistic healers varies enormously from people who cannot bring in additional perceptions and levels of consciousness to giants such as Clive Harris and Matthew Manning whose healing is very broad and deep; but they all have one thing in common, Universe Consciousness, which gives them the ability to bring about systemic change. To heal the perceptions and levels of consciousness the healer needs Spirit Consciousness or the ability to get the necessary help 'over the air' from some healer with Spirit Consciousness or from the holistic healing network. For beginners and healers with little power the paramount need is for their level of consciousness 4 (fellow workers) to be opened, as it commonly is in wild animals and people living a more simple life than most of us. The next great step is for level of consciousness 8 to be opened as wide as is right, so that the healer can get support from his 'brothers and sisters' for healing and for everyday life. The state of our Being varies from day to day according to the strength of our constitutions and the demands made on us in our healing work and ordinary activities. When elements of the Being fail for some reason it is these 'brothers and sisters; who come to our aid. Much depression and feelings of loneliness are due to insufficient support from this source.

Healing is accomplished by proximity radiations, by distant healing beams and the transmission of healing energies by touch and hand. None can be achieved unless our perception 8 (spirits) is open because healing can only take place with the help of the spirit world. This does not mean to say that healers have to be spiritualists. For most of us this perception is blocked by fear in the Soul. Some people have amazing proximity powers; John Caine can open up level of consciousness 10 (future) in a room full of people merely by stretching out his hands, but for me the greatest proximity healer must be the present Pope. When addressing a vast audience he cleanses the Beings of the vast majority and opens up their levels of consciousness 9 (right path) with the result that increasingly they get right path guidance in their daily lives. Great artists and entertainers have great proximity gifts. Vladimir Ashkenazy can heal the Spirit and Tom Jones the Soul by proximity. A great proximity healer has a very different para-sympathetic nervous system from most of us in that he has thousands of nerves emitting, unconsciously, radiations and beams as needed. Great hand healers also have special constitutions to enable them to heal people with different constitutions. Anyone who has Soul Consciousness can hand heal to some extent by placing their hand or hands on the right spot for a time. The prime result is to clear emotional or worry blocks from level of consciousness 3 (family and friends). This results in some physical repairs being started. To repair organs or tissues the healer must have Universe Consciousness. This enables the healer to get help via perception 10 from other healers and healing networks. Touch healing can heal the Earth, Nature and Universe Bodies thus setting in train systemic and functional change so that the patient moves in time to a higher mode of Being with a superior constitution and expanded awareness. There is another form of healing which is beyond me to analyse, when by proximity or distant healing the healer is able, unconsciously, to ask for healing spirits to heal the patient direct. Distant healing, in which dowsers are very strong, is accomplished in many ways: in radionics it is done with the aid of apparatus, by visualisation and by the use of models of some sort. Many hand and touch healers give unconscious distant healing before they see or know of their patients; sometimes it may be years in advance, and they can continue to give unconscious distant healing after an actual meeting.

Some healers will find that they will be able to heal the levels of consciousness and perception at the right time by touch. Healing in this way psychological blocks are cleared and any necessary physical repairs will be put to hand. No further conscious healing is necessary. There is no need to consider the physical body at all; the necessary physical healing is done by spirits. With a few exceptions this type of healing has not been possible since the 'fall'. Healers who can heal in this way will have Spirit Consciousness, sub-level of consciousness 10 and perception 8 (spirits) in service. Needless to say the touch healing will have been preceded by a period of unconscious distant healing. For many healers the final stage in their healing will occur when their sub-level of consciousness 7 (patients), comes into service. When this is available, at the right time, when a certain amount of work has been done, patients will be placed in the patient category when they will become the responsibility of the holistic healing or some specialist network.

Sometimes the benefits of healing can be swift and dramatic but often it is a lengthy business because with holistic healing, invariably, there will be major physical changes as the body gradually sorts itself out for better functioning. This is particularly the case with elderly people where much wear and tear and some of the results of what we regard as natural ageing have to be made good. It should often be possible to help what may seem to be a hopeless situation by giving comfort and easing pain. Pain is always caused by incoming Sun energies going astray. Relief can be given by finding the entry point and blocking it by touch healing. This is the case with all pain including headaches. Blocking the incoming energy should not be regarded as an admission of defeat; it is part of the natural healing process. When the necessary physical changes have taken place, the energy will be restored in its proper channel.

Apart from physical benefits, healing can do much for adverse conditions such as depression, shock and emotional problems. An interesting benefit is improved muscular co-ordination which results as the Sun Body and level of consciousness 10 and the spleen are working well resulting in an effective function 4. One of the many problems caused by an ineffective function 4 is that common condition, a bad back. Most of us have to develop new skills by receiving instruction and by hard work, but we all know people who were born with a gift for a particular activity involving muscular and digital skills. What they have are first class functioning of the sensory and control, muscular activity and co-ordination, and the reason, thinking and imagination functions. Then there are the virtuoso musicians. In addition to the physical attributes they have the gift of perceiving and expressing beauty.

Apart from the benefits to people and animals by healing made possible by the new energies and expanded consciousness, there are much wider implications for all forms of life on earth. As more people receive the gift of cleansing so the cleansing of the earth, trees and plants will be speeded up. Many healers will find that in addition to their ordinary healing work they have special responsibilities for particular animals, trees or plants. Insecticides will begin to be a thing of the past when people find, as Dr Marcel Vogel knows, that it is possible for man to communicate with offending animals and insects, and by thought ask them to go away. As this cleaning up process gets under way, more energies will get through to the earth and growing things, and our need for the use of artificial fertilisers will reduce. Expanded consciousness will enable dowsers to locate unlimited supplies of underground water, which hitherto only a handful of dowsers have been able to find. I believe also that in the near future we will find ways of producing heat and electricity from the unlimited Universe energy. Man at several times in prehistory has enjoyed these gifts and many more. The rate at which these great changes come in will depend on the effectiveness of holistic healers. Healing in the way described in this book not only initiates systemic change when necessary to clear many chronic problems but it can make good much 'daily wear and tear', and in the case of healers can clear undesirable elements which may have been picked up in the course of their healing work. It is most desirable therefore that healers should meet with healing friends from time to time so that they can give each other healing as necessary. The ideal technique for such occasions is the Metamorphic Technique which is described in the next section. It is stressed that healing is not just to clear pains or undesirable symptoms, it is concerned with the proper development of the Being and whilst it would be rare for people other than healers to look at it in this light, healers should have the opportunity to get regular healing from friends with this end in mind.

My Healing Routines

Since I started healing I have never had any difficulty in making distant contact with patients and my fellow-healers who support me in all my healing work. Some healers need a witness, such as a lock of hair, but I have never found this to be necessary. When I began I made copious notes but now I make no notes at all; I do not even keep a list of patients. I start a distant healing session by asking 'is there work to be done?' If the answer is yes, which it usually is, I have to find out who needs help. This I can do very quickly by asking such questions as 'is it a man?', 'is he to the north or south?' etc. Having identified the subject I have to find out step by step what I must do. Sometimes the contact is sufficient but if that is not the case I may have to clear redundant chakras or bring chakras or levels of consciousness into service. It may be anything. Whenever my healing range increases any patient I have treated benefits if it is appropriate for him to do so. Usually this is an unconscious process but sometimes I have to go back several years to identify the right patient. The help of my fellow-healers is available whenever I need it. This is also an unconscious process but sometimes out of curiosity I will find out who has been helping me with a particular problem. Some of my fellow-healers are personal friends but some I have never met. Some are, on the face of it, very ordinary people, whereas some are well-known figures; one helper is Mother Teresa. A major development in recent months has been the establishment of the worldwide holistic network which gives support to any holistic healer and to their patients. From time to time I meet people who tell me they work with me daily or occasionally. These are some of my fellow-workers in various stages of development. Similarly many fellow-workers help and guide me during conscious lessons. Sometimes when I am working I have a flurry of remedy taking, usually for the benefit of a patient. Until recently I have used very frequently Oil of Olbas, Pakua and the Bach Rescue Remedy by dabbing a spot of one or more on my hands or face to clear perception blockages.

My work has been made easy in many ways. I learned the morse code in my army days so when I was stuck for a word I could spell it out with the pendulum, clockwise and anti-clockwise gyrations representing dots and dashes respectively. Just after I started healing a friend asked me if I could do something for his dog. The pendulum spelled out 'suffusion of the kidneys'. I took this to mean that it was taking more water than its kidneys could deal with. I told him this, he cut down its water intake and the dog got better, recovering the use of its back leg-muscles. Although I had not done so consciously, I subsequently found that I had given it distant healing. Not long after that stage the forefinger of my left hand began to tap out words in morse. This together with a measure of clairaudience enables me to work very quickly. For the past four years I have rarely had to use the pendulum for dowsing. I am able to dowse with my Mind since my level of consciousness 6 came good. Now when I need a remedy I just pick it out of the box, not bothering to read the label. There is no point in doing so as the properties of remedies vary with the power of the healer. If I want a book I just walk to the bookshelf and pick it up. Usually it opens at the right page and my finger points to the passage I need.

Every phase of my distant healing work always has an objective beyond the welfare of the patient I am treating.

Sometimes I have to give conscious attention to some energy centre, sometimes the further objective is to initiate the cleansing of some remote ground, but mostly it is to do with bringing superior systems and functions into being, because that is the only way that many people can be healed of many physical, psychological and emotional problems. The most difficult one on which I have been consciously involved is bringing into service the new lymph system to which I have referred elsewhere. The final block I had to clear was jealousy from the Universe level of consciousness.

When I began to hand heal I would find out via the pendulum where and for how long to place my hands, sometimes for quite long periods, but now most of my healing is accomplished by touch, usually on the hands and fingers, face and neck. This clears allergies caused by Mind blockages in the brain. It can also clear blockages which are halting necessary systemic and functional change. To block a wrong energy intake I may hold my finger about half an inch away from the skin for up to three or four minutes. Sometimes I have no need to touch a patient apart from shaking hands; the healing is accomplished by my proximity and the distant help of fellow-healers. I have no need to ask for such assistance as it is always available when needed. All healers get this type of help but few are aware of it. When hand or touch healing no conscious thought is needed; as with the selection of remedies my hands and fingers know exactly what to do. This is one of the many gifts healers are given.

The major strand running through my work for the past seven years has been the development of the model of the Possible Human Being. The whole of this book has been written almost entirely from the intuition. None of the information I gained was from a book or as the result of a conventional research approach. I gained knowledge as I worked. Each step forward marked the end of one aspect of my healing work and they were all hard won. The most

important revelation was that available to man were ten
major etheric bodies, levels of consciousness and perception. Many healers work on the basis of seven etheric bodies
in accordance with the Indian tradition. The fact that there
are three more levels available for more and more people has
enormous implications for man's physical well-being, his
happiness and for the flora and fauna of the earth.

I recently came across the Metamorphic Technique
which clears prenatal blocks by massage of the feet, hands
and head. I find that it clears Level 1 of the Bodies which
carry the genetic pattern and are not amenable to my
method. The embryo is subjected to many hazards which
can damage the genetic pattern such as many modern drugs,
family arguments and violence causing adverse conditions
such as Down's syndrome, dyslexia and many others. The
most commonly damaged levels are Water, Nature, Spirit
and Cosmic. Apart from the serious conditions there are
many which are not recognised, such as blocked non-physical functions. Most commonly affected are the cleansing,
energising and protection. I have found that the technique is
absolutely complementary to my own method and now it is
the first treatment I give. The technique is fully described in
The Metamorphic Technique by Gaston St. Pierre and Debbie
Boater, published by Element Books.

A fascinating aspect of my work over the past four years
has been running or participating in workshops. This gift
appeared when I attained Universe Consciousness. Until
recently, when starting a workshop, I was unable to 'see' the
objective, but now that I can it is no longer a matter of
working blind. As in all my work I proceed on the basis of
'what shall I do now?' I am able at every step to know who
needs healing and who should give it. Sometimes those
concerned can do their own thing, at other times I have to
give them some assistance, telling them where to place their
hands or fingers and for how long. Working in this way one
gets the optimum healing for those present and the right

path for the main objective. Invariably, early on in a session most of the work is directed to opening up levels of consciousness and perception, but as the work proceeds systemic change is initiated. Thus for the individuals concerned the major physical benefits are often long term but they very quickly get the advantage of increased vitalities which enhance their own healing powers. Subsequently, however, much of the work they do is unconscious; not until they acquire Soul Consciousness are they able to know the nature of the work they are unconsciously doing. The workshops and the subsequent healing development of those present is under the guidance of the Cosmic Spirit. One immediate result of these workshops is that all those present are opened up to level of consciousness 4 (fellow-workers), that is healers. This means that in their individual healing work they get automatic and unconscious assistance from the others. It is a very powerful method of healing.

I ran a very beautiful workshop near Brussels in 1980. The venue was an old house in the forest, appropriately named Le Source because it is a Water 5 and Nature 5 energy centre. The fifteen present were all followers of Paul Soloman's Inner Light movement. During the workshop, which ran over two days, I was guided to play some music – part of Beethoven's 9th Symphony, Schubert's Quintet in C Major and Nana Mouskouri singing The Spinning Wheel. In that setting the music constituted an invitation to three great spirits, Universe 10, Spirit 10 and Soul 10 respectively to join us at the appropriate time. There was no need to invite the Cosmic Spirit, he was in charge throughout.

Towards the end of the second day one of the party, a Dutchman, had to sit in the centre of the circle to receive healing from the Cosmic Spirit. After a while he passed into a state of deep meditation during which I was guided to go outside for a few minutes. When I returned all the others were around him with hands on heads, shoulders and hands. After about half an hour he emerged from the meditation, having had the most wonderful visualisations. One of the many things which happened during that sequence was the establishment of a channel from Le Source to Trafalgar Square for the transmission of Water and Nature 5 energies. They were last generally available 2,000 years ago.

The Healing Methods

The healing methods detailed below are all holistic in that they relate to the whole Being and its relationship with our greater environment. Any healing is given to the right individual at the 'hour in time.' It is not haphazard. It is controlled by the holistic network of incarnate and spirit healers under the overall control of the Universe Spirit. It is a long time since such a network was available to mankind. A huge increase in man's healing powers is presently appearing as miasms – blockages caused by disease residues – are being cleared from people, animals, vegetation and the earth. These miasms impair our wisdom, range of consciousness and vitality. Many people can use the first nine methods. The extent to which anyone can use them will depend largely on the individual's state of Being. The only skill needed is the ability to 'find' the person needing help and the method to be used, by dowsing. Method 11 can only be used by people whose level of consciousness Universe 9 is open. Anyone applying any of the methods will be able to get some feedback so that they will have the satisfaction of knowing that they have done something useful by checking how many chakras have been, or are in the process of being, brought into service.

 Method 1, although very simple, is very powerful. Recently I showed a beginner how to use it and his first essay resulted in twenty-two chakras being brought into service two months later, two for his friend, one for himself, two for me and the remainder for a number of people and one dog.

METHOD 1

At any spare moment ask if there is work to be done. If the answer is yes find out by question and answer who needs help by asking such questions as 'is it a man?' or 'is it a woman?' 'Is he or she to the north of me? to the south? to the east? or to the west? Is he or she young or old?' With practice you will find this is very easy. I can usually identify the subject within two or three shots. Having found your subject allow the pendulum to move until it stops. It will gyrate and may jump about quite a lot. Each sequence will usually stop within one minute, indicating that the treatment is in hand. Repeat the procedure for others until you have completed the run or until you have to stop because there is something else you have to do. Although this is very simple, working in this way you will be linking up your patients with the appropriate healing network at the right time. Most of us try to send healing and comfort by thought to friends or relatives who are ill or in some sort of trouble, but these thoughts are rarely helpful because usually we think of them when they are unable to receive our thoughts, and also we are lucky if we are able by chance to make contact with the appropriate healing network. It is no good allowing oneself to be influenced by conscious feelings or emotions and asking at random for help for someone we know is sick or in some sort of trouble. Some people, particularly the elderly, many find after a successful session that it may be days or weeks before they get the O.K. for another. This is because anyone using this method will also receive healing if they need it from an appropriate network, and non-physical or physical changes may be put in hand which prevent them from healing for a while.

METHOD 2

This is a method which may be helpful to experienced healers as well as to beginners. It corrects the magnetic field of the patient and by so doing brings into service non-physical connections that had been lost. It can be regarded as a treatment for shock. I have one fine healer friend who has been able to use this for many years and it is the first treatment he gives to any patient. He says seven people out of ten need nothing else. The very high success rate may, however, be due to his other great healing powers. The method is as follows. With the left hand hold the patient's left hand and cause the pendulum, held in the right hand, to gyrate rapidly. If you cannot sense when the treatment is complete, pause and ask if more is needed.

METHOD 3

The fact that this method can be used by a significant number of people is because a miasm, Spirit 8, is in the process of being cleared. The miasm was caused by tuberculosis. As it clears, a new healing energy, Soul 7, is being made available to more people. This was last widespread about 30,000 years ago. For it to be manifest a new vitality has to appear. This happens when the respiratory system and function change so that the lungs can extract a subtle energy from the Air field. It was known to the Indians as prana. Prana is and always has been available: our great athletes use it. It is beneficial for all the functions. Loss of the gift was to protect us from cancer which was endemic as recently as two thousand years ago. This is the method. After using Method 2 place both hands on the patient's shoulders for up to ten minutes. It cleanses Mind, Soul, Spirit, Cosmic and Universe Bodies.

METHOD 4

Sometimes when distant healing with Method 1, healers may find that a name is indicated but they are unable to get the person connected to a healing network. This always means that the healer knows someone who can connect the patient to the appropriate network. The method is to find that person and then proceed as in Method 1.

METHOD 5

Place the left hand on the back of the patient's neck and hold the patient's right hand with the right hand for as long as necessary, which may be as long as five minutes. This corrects faulty perceptions.

METHOD 6

Place the left hand on top of the patient's head and hold the patient's right hand with the right hand for as long as necessary which may be up to five minutes. This corrects faulty levels of consciousness.

METHOD 7

Place both hands on top of the patient's head for up to ten minutes. This corrects faulty levels of understanding.

METHOD 8

Place both hands at the back of the patient's head for up to ten minutes. This corrects faulty levels of knowledge.

METHOD 9

Place both hands on the patient's shoulder-blades for up to ten minutes. This corrects faulty chakras.

METHOD 10

Place both hands at the top of the patient's chest for up to ten minutes. This corrects faulty bodies.

METHOD 11

If the pendulum has indicated that you can help someone but that none of the above methods are appropriate it means that you have to get guidance from a higher intelligence using the method described previously. Quite simply, this means starting work with an empty mind and finding out step by step what has to be done. You may be guided to examine diet, to refer the patient to some other therapy or to refer to the work sheets. It is not possible to give further guidance because the possible field of work is so vast. Needed for this method are imagination and diligence. Any session will usually include help to people suffering from mental, emotional or psychic problems.

One of the great advantages of working in this way is that the healer does not need the patient to tell him what the problem is, which is just as well because how many people know the cause of their problems. Many people are severely handicapped by the fear of death but are unaware of it. As Paracelsus wrote:

"If a physician knows nothing more about his patient than what the latter tells him, he knows very little indeed, because the patient usually knows only that he suffers pain. Nature causes and cures diseases, and it is therefore necessary that the physician should know the processes of Nature, the invisible as well as the visible man. He will then be able to recognise the cause and the course of a disease, and he will know much more by using his own reason than by all that the looks or the patient may tell him. Medical science may be acquired by learning, but medical wisdom is given by God."

A Few Brief Case Histories

Now that my healing model is complete and my perceptions and levels of consciousness are in reasonably good order, by using the model I can reconstruct healing events as far back in time as I need to go! Indeed from time to time I have had to look into previous incarnations of patients and clear problems resulting from disease, traumatic experiences and changes in environmental energies. Until recently, as is the case with most healers, I have had to work in the dark, but now as I have said, before starting a healing session I can often ascertain its objective. This is very useful as it reduces the likelihood of stopping work before all that can be done is done.

The following analyses illustrate the use of the model and its credibility. Poisoning of some sort and psychic aggression feature in many cases. One patient was a middle-aged lady who had been in and out of mental hospitals for twenty years. I gave her hand healing on two occasions. Six years later she has had no recurrence of the problem, which was caused by failure of kidneys in function 6 (reason) and failure of the spleen in function 10 (protection). I was able to put the necessary repairs in hand because of an unusual energy I had, Cosmic 1. I have had that all my life. I can see that I have unconsciously given similar healing to a number of people affected in the same way by touch and proximity.

A woman in her early fifties had suffered for some years from intense attacks of depression and was getting little from life. From time to time over the years I had been able to help her but had not been able to effect a cure. Her main problem was poor protection due to an ineffective Earth Body which had made her vulnerable to psychic aggression. She had been a target for many years because she had a latent gift for dealing with such aggression. On her last visit I was able to give her special protection. She has since used her great gift to good effect.

A middle-aged man who had back trouble and whose protection was poor was another patient. I gave him healing on several occasions and the problem which had bothered him for many years cleared up. Friends remarked on how well he was looking. The problem originated in his Earth Body when chakra 2 became blocked on a visit to Stonehenge. This led to malfunctioning of the spleen in function 4 (muscular activity and coordination). My key energy in healing him was Universe 1. The sequence of repairs was as follows: repair to his kidneys in sexual function 5, a brain change which resulted in his function 4 moving to the proper part of his brain thus clearing his self-repair capability.

A middle-aged woman had suffered severely from osteoarthritis for some years. Her mobility was very poor. By distant healing I was able to bring about a vast improvement within a few weeks, so much so that within a month she phoned me to say she had been shopping and on arriving home she realised that she had run all the way back. On the face of it the arthritis had been precipitated by an accident in which she had been injured, but an important contributary factor had been the presence of arsenic in her body tissues. Physically three organs had failed, her spleen in function 4 (muscular activity and coordination) the pancreas in function 5 (sexual) and the gall-bladder in function 10, (protection). I succeeded because I had the gift of clearing arsenic by distant healing. I lost the gift a few months later as a result of psychic attack but I am glad to say it returned.

I also treated a young woman who had been unwell for some years and very ill for several months. When I first saw her she was writhing in agony in bed. I do not know what the clinical diagnosis of her problem was. I was only able to touch her face and hands but I gave hand healing to her mother. My touch healing cleared a group of radiation allergies such as plastics and stone. Her root problem was in her gall–bladder in function 10 (protection). In the long period she had been unwell several organs had been damaged, her stomach in her function 3 (elimination) her bowel in the same function and her left lung in her function 5 (sexual). Her mother unconsciously completed the healing by proximity. She was feeling in splendid form within a week.

An elderly friend had gangrene in his leg and when I saw him had just been told that the leg would have to be amputated within two weeks. I gave him touch healing on several occasions and cleared many allergies to food, beverages and radiations from his environment. The origin of the trouble was that, as a child, he visited Winchester Cathedral and was opened to Cosmic 5 in the wrong channel, in function 9 (energising). This caused lack of maintenance in his circulation system with the result that arterio–sclerosis had become a significant problem fifty years later. His leg was not amputated.

An elderly man who had been suffering for some years from disseminated sclerosis was another patient. The objective of the first session was to heal his Water Body 3 which was in a very poor condition with the result that his blood contained masses of disease residues from the initial attack. This occurred when he was opened to Air 3 in the wrong channel, Nature 3. This caused two major allergies, to bread and silica in the earth. I believe these could have been stopped at an early date by blocking the offending Air 3 by touch healing the hands. Further healing would have been necessary to give him protection until the root cause – arsenic poisoning and psychic aggression – was eliminated.

His Body 3 was healed in the first session and began to generate the necessary vitalities. He was put on a course of feverfew tablets and a good diet. The allergies were cleared and his pain was stopped. There was no need to take any action about the poisoning or aggression. It was taken care of by the Universe Spirit. Full recovery is going to take a long time because many repairs have to take place but an improvement was apparent within a week. Apart from the improvement in his physical condition and mobility his new healing, cleansing and protection functions were brought into service.

I met an elderly man at a drinks party who told me that he was suffering from hiatus hernia. There and then, by thought, I blocked the offending energy, Air 1, and told him to keep off sugar for a few weeks. The next time I saw him the problem had gone and he was feeling fine. Three years later he has had no recurrence. I understand that sometimes sufferers from this complaint undergo a horrendous operation.

A friend had an agonising pain in his back, so great that he was frightened to move from his chair. The pain reduced considerably when I gave him hand healing on his legs and cleared completely in a day or two. His trouble was caused by a black magic and witchcraft attack which caused some Cosmic energies to be diverted from his suspensory ligaments and tendons to the muscles of his back. The hand healing cleared the bad influence, the product of the attack, and novocaine which had weakened his protection. The pain was caused by an alarm energy, Sun 1.

A woman whose protection was very poor came to see me. I did not enquire about any physical problems she may have had. She had been married to a man who had beaten her unmercifully. The good offices of well-meaning counsellors and other agencies had kept them together until one day her doctor uttered these immortal words, 'Leave the beggar now,' which she did and was much happier for

doing so. At one stage I told her that she had to send a
healing thought to her husband, to which she replied 'I
won't.' I said she must, whereupon she said 'I can't.' To my
amazement I was able, by thought, to make her do so
because her spirit wanted to. She had to get rid of that
grudge! She had to forgive him!

Landmarks in Man's Development

The main changes that have affected man, and indeed all life on this planet, are changes in the environmental fields and cataclysmic and climatic changes. Each of these has affected in some degree man's constitution to enable him to survive in the changed environment with its changed flora and fauna and its new diseases. The cataclysmic and climatic events such as periods of intense seismic activity, intense heat and cold, massive rainfall and drought, obviously necessitated great changes in his way of life, but changes in the great fields brought about subtle but no less important changes in his perceptions, consciousness and attributes. Although at some periods we have been superior to our present condition and at other periods inferior, the general trend, with many setbacks, has been towards happier lives with extended awareness so that we see more clearly our responsibilities towards each other and for all other forms of life on earth. Each major change has presented us with the opportunity to learn another lesson. Man has been on the earth a very long time but it is sufficient for my present purpose to recall from the akashic records – a record of everything that is and ever has been – a few of the major landmarks since and including the 'fall'.

The fall occurred about 30,000 years ago when we were opened to a new energy, Cosmic 1. This found its way into the wrong energy channel, Nature 1. The result was endemic syphilis. Those who survived did so with a much inferior lymph system and with impaired energy, elimination, sexual, reason and cleansing functions. Life expectancy and the quality of life were much reduced and we became open to feelings of shame. Up to that time people had lived communally but afterwards monogamy began to be the norm.

The next major event in Europe was a period of great cold which intensified over about a hundred years. Many moved to warmer climes but a fair number stayed and adapted to the new conditions. Man had to live almost exclusively on meat whereas previously his diet had been more mixed. This new diet brought about major digestive changes. The small intestine increased in size so that food could be more fully digested. There was more competition for the available nourishment and to survive man had to become more ruthless. His sense of responsibility, level of consciousness 1, towards his fellow-man reduced. His protection against wrong Nature energies was also reduced so that he became more susceptible to a number of infectious diseases.

About 10,000 years ago the Mind field reduced in strength. This caused a reduction in intuition and guidance which forced man to think more in order to live, and set in train a vast increase in what we regard today as intelligence. In other words he had to rely more on physical senses and deductive processes.

The Biblical flood occurred about 6,000 years ago. Most of Europe was affected by it. The appalling resultant diet meant that his vitality had to be used for life support and non-essential gifts had to be curtailed. Most people lost their gifts of touch and proximity healing which necessarily led to an interest in healing-herbs and medicines.

About 4,000 years ago the Soul field reduced. This caused a reduction in Soul 7, which brought about an onset of cruelty and indifference to human and animal suffering.

2,000 years ago, coincident with the birth of Mary, there was a great increase in Spirit. This brought about the attribute of unconditional love in a few people. For the majority it had an adverse effect on Mind which was the inability to foresee intuitively the result of their actions and a loss of their reasoning power. Sixteen years later the birth of Christ coincided with the appearance of a new energy, Cosmic 10. For people who were properly opened to it this gave protection against psychic aggression which had been widespread since the fall. It also gave the ability to heal energy levels 6 and 7 of the Soul which had rarely been possible for many years. People with these levels working were needed so that by proximity and touch healing they could begin the spread of Cosmic Consciousness which is now becoming a dominant factor in determining our future. Cosmic Consciousness can clear prejudice, meaningless convention and indifference from the world.

A new energy, Cosmic 5, appeared about 1,500 years ago. Most people were blocked to it but the few who were opened to it were given the gift of healing level of consciousness 1 (obligations) which was spread by proximity and touch. As the years went by more and more people began to take a broader view of their responsibilities, and to be aware of the needs of people other than their family and friends. Today the miasm which has been blocking the widespread distribution of that energy is being cleared, so that we will see in the near future an increase in the sense of responsibility in an increasing number of people.

In the twelfth century AD there was an increase in the strength of the Spirit field. This had the effect of opening wider level of consciousness 4 (fellow-workers). This not only referred to people working together in the ordinary way, but also to people working unconsciously together on a great healing network, the object of which was to open up more and more people to level of consciousness 9, (right path), who came increasingly under Divine guidance.

600 years ago there was a decrease in the Sun field. This caused a reduction in our cleansing function which resulted

in the blocking by discarnates of some Cosmic and Universe energies. Our protection against a number of infectious diseases was weakened, in particular the one known as Black Death which today we know as influenza. On the credit side however, level of consciousness 4 and perception 8 opened wider in many people who thus began to receive more unconscious support from their fellow-men and from the spirit world.

In the seventeenth century a new energy appeared, Universe 5. This opened up perception 5 (diet and remedies) and 9 (plants, trees, animals and humans in need of help). More people became aware of the need for a better diet, and doctors and healers became more effective as their knowledge of herbs and remedies increased.

Another new energy appeared in the eighteenth century, Water 9, which brought with it for many Bubonic plague. Those who survived did so with an impaired urinary system which caused inadequate cleansing of toxins from the blood and a reduction in energies for Mind. Intuition decreased.

The explosion of the first atom bombs started massive changes in many people who became open for the first time since the fall to Soul 8. This initiated changes in the three nervous systems which led to the major systemic and functional changes which are the theme of this book. Since then ten new energies have been becoming widely available which are having a vast and beneficial effect in that an increasing number of people are receiving Cosmic Consciousness.

For anyone who can verify these landmarks by dowsing or who knows intuitively that they are true, the meaning must be that the ups and downs we experience individually and collectively are not the result of original sin; it is just that things happen to us. As the Universe, our Cosmos and our Earth change so do environment and our Spirit. As I see it the big lesson we have had to learn since the fall is tolerance. The greatest block to that is belief in the concept of original sin. When that goes, Cosmic Consciousness comes in.

The Three Great Gifts
Wisdom, Love and Vitality

These gifts were once common amongst mankind but now-adays they are very rare. They were lost a long time ago before the fall when most of mankind was opened to a new energy, Cosmic 7. For the vast majority this found its way into the wrong channel, Nature 7, and caused epidemic and endemic smallpox. Those who survived did so with inferior urinary and circulation systems and impaired functions. A very small number of people received the energy in the proper channel which had previously been blocked. They attained Cosmic Consciousness and with it the three gifts. It was the responsibility of these few to help mankind to survive in its enfeebled state and this they have continued to do until the present day. From time to time they have surfaced as coherent groups such as Essenes, Druids and Cathars, and now as members of the Holistic Healing Network, a body with no list of members, no meetings, in fact with no earthly organisation. The network began to coalesce in 1948 after some people received energy Cosmic 3 as a result of radioactive fallout. For these people the long process of systemic change began, accompanied by increased perceptions and expanded consciousness. The task of the network which became active six years ago is to help healers, regardless of religion, school or discipline to ease their patients smoothly through systemic change so that they acquire superior constitutions with expanded awareness. It is only with expanded awareness that we can perceive and receive help from the spirit world. Many of the healers doing this are unaware of the fact.

Shortly before completing this book I picked from the bookshelf *Tertium Organum,* by P.D. Ouspensky, a great mathematician, philosopher and mystic and a colleague of Gurdjieff. The basic argument of the book is that the real world is not the one we perceive with our physical senses; the real world is the invisible noumenal world. From my work over the past six years I am convinced that it is in the noumenal world that events take place leading to physical manifestations. For right things to happen, to fulfil our proper destiny, that is to be happy, we must accept the plans and decisions which have already been made in the noumenal world with our unconscious participation. As I began to read, Ouspensky came through as a great spirit and told me that he had taken over Mind level of consciousness 6 in many people throughout the world and had used it for the establishment of the Holistic Healing Network. In almost everyone that level had been blocked since the smallpox epidemic referred to above. In the intervening years that channel had been used by the Universe Spirit, who has responsibility for all life, to open up in many people, by proximity, distant healing and touch, perception 8 (spirits) and level of consciousness 10 (future) so that they could cooperate with the spirit world and foresee a world where there would be increasing harmony between people and with the greater nature kingdom, because right things can only happen if we can foresee them, and to do that we need to cooperate with the spirit kingdom.

Wisdom has nothing to do with cleverness or book learning. It has all to do with imagination and open-mindedness. The biggest block to wisdom is pride in the Spirit, the feeling that if we try hard enough we can accomplish whatever we have decided to do. Pride is in setting targets and pressing on relentlessly to achieve them, though interim events and changes in one's own Being make them pointless. Wisdom is acting one step at a time, having no targets and making decisions at the right moment. Wisdom cannot be exercised unless we have access to the relevant sensory and perceived data and the right levels of consciousness to enable us to make the right decisions in any given situation. God is our guide but, as he is in everything, the extent of the guidance depends on the extent to which we have consciousness of his works. This comes with consciousness of the great Spirits. With Universe Consciousness the gift of true healing is given, with Nature Consciousness the gift of 'green fingers' and with Earth Consciousness the gift of physical energy. Sometimes we hear people say "God is my guide"; well, of course he is, who else? But people with only two or three main levels of consciousness will not be able to live a full life. In the Western world most of us have access to God through Water, Nature, Soul and Earth. The body which has the task of processing all the acquired data and knowledge is Mind. For this job to be done properly adequate Mind vitality is necessary. This is often inadequate because of an inferior urinary system when control is exercised by the wrong part of the brain, resulting in subtle energy deficiency.

Love is the great healing energy. It is positive and makes us feel happy. Hatred is negative and makes us unhappy, and contaminates people, animals, plants, trees, buildings and articles. This contamination can subsequently be picked up, with undesirable consequences, by people with inadequate protection. Each body should generate love on level 7, but for most of us only three or four levels are functioning, Earth, Water, Nature and more rarely Soul. Moreover, the healing function is usually partially blocked so that the output is even more attenuated. People are attracted by others who emit levels in which they themselves are deficient. The great proximity healers such as the late Albert

Schweizer, the pianist Vladimir Ashkenazy and Mother
Teresa dispense love unconditionally to all and everything.
People normally emitting love on three or four levels may in
the presence of certain people emit several more. The most
extreme example of this is when a man and woman fall in
love. This is because in most of us there is a mix up between
the sexual and healing functions so that the love outputs are
only triggered by sexual attraction. This is why for many
marriage is such a fragile arrangement because loss of
mutual sexuality may mean loss of mutual love. All levels of
love are vulnerable to hostility and negative emotions unless
there is Cosmic and Universe Consciousness. When these
levels of consciousness have been attained the act of love,
like our unconscious processes, comes under the direct
control of God and becomes the supreme blissful experience. There is no question of planning or contriving such
unions. If it is right that it should happen it will happen.

Vitalities are subtle energies needed for proper functioning. They may be derived from food or from the environment fields. Until Universe Consciousness is attained few
people can have adequate vitalities because they depend on
right systems which are rare. In this country typical vitalities for a man of fifty are:

Earth 3/10, Air 1/10, Water 5/10, Sun 2/10, Nature 5/10,
Mind 2/10, Soul 6/10, Spirit 2/10, Cosmic 0, Universe 0.

The result is that some functions are almost completely
ineffective. Typical figures for the functions of a man of
fifty are:

Energy 6/10, Sensory and Control 6/10, Elimination 6/10,
Muscular 5/10, Sexual 2/10, Thinking etc. 2/10, Healing
1/10, Cleansing 1/10, Energising 4/10 and Protection 3/10.

Readers may wonder how people can get by with such
poor functioning. The short answer is by conventions. By
staying on well trodden paths, by being careful about
everything and by being fearful about many things. There
have been times in the past when less technologically

advanced cultures have had much greater vitality and have been happier and healthier than we are. A startling change however occurs with Universe Consciousness. Our vitalities cease to be dependent on our physical systems and will operate at whatever level is required in any given situation. Our physical functions such as muscular activity depend also of course on our glands and constitution, but some functions viz thinking, healing, cleansing, energising and protection cease to do so. This means that frail people who have Universe Consciousness can still do great work. It further means that people with Universe Consciousness can achieve a superior physical constitution more quickly than would otherwise be the case.

It is no good anyone trying directly to acquire these gifts. They may be given during healing of some sort or they may be given as a result of right work which may be by doing healing work or repairing roads.

Personal Insights

With my present sensitivity I have been able to look back at a number of events and experiences in my life and see the connecting thread that led to my present involvement in healing. I was a sickly child. I had everything that was going, measles, chicken-pox, scarlet fever and mumps. When I was three years old I had what the doctor said were abscesses between the scalp and the bone. In fact it was cancer of the scalp. The doctor did not cure it; he healed it. The cancer was the reaction to a new energy, Cosmic 1. This energy put in train brain changes in my para-sympathetic nervous system that led to my present sensitivity. When I was seven years old I got peritonitis. In those days appendicitis was a serious complaint but peritonitis was usually fatal. In fact I went through to 'the other side' and came back with a new level of consciousness, Nature 1. This put in train brain and systemic changes which seven years ago manifested in a gift which enabled me, by touch, to help people who were unwell because their lymph systems were unsuccessfully trying to move to a higher state of functioning.

In my early teens I had many prophetic dreams, usually relating to events of little importance, but one in particular stayed in my memory. I dreamed I was looking up at the night sky and saw all the stars rhythmically swinging to and fro. During the dream I thought it was silly, because if the earth was moving like that all man-made structures would be destroyed. Fourteen years later, on a troop-ship steaming through tropical waters. I was asleep on deck and woke up to see all the stars swinging rhythmically to and fro in the sky. That was when my Being opened to Universe Consciousness. That started a process which, when I began to heal, enabled me to clear fear from the soul of some people. There was a related event seven years ago when I was attending a Wrekin Trust seminar being run by Maxwell Cade, the great researcher into levels of consciousness. I was connected up to his Mind Mirror, an electrical device which makes brain patterns visible on an array of small lamps. Whilst I was connected up, Max's wife, Isobel, asked me to think of a woman present who was very unhappy. I did so and it was found that I had clocked up a pattern in the form of a letter 'O'. The only 'O' they had seen before was registered by Sir George Trevelyan. I am sure that many more have been clocked up since. Whilst I was connected up I was opened to a new level of consciousness and energy, Water 1. This has enabled me to help people who are having problems when Spirit 5 opens and is unprotected. The two events are related because those energies and levels of consciousness are needed to enable the digestive and defecation systems to split for the generation of new vitalities.

In 1943 at the Roshenara Club in Old Delhi I met a beautiful young Indian woman, Bani. She was the friend of an army friend I was with, and she was standing us dinner because I think we were broke. I subsequently met her in Calcutta at her engagement party, and in Oxford at the wedding of the friend I had been with at the Roshenara Club. Bani and I have not met since 1950 but I now realise that we have been partners since our first meeting, working at some level to prepare for the time when mankind would be given the gift of healing human and animal etheric bodies presently blocking Cosmic energies from the earth. The last time such a healing programme was put in hand was about 30,000 years ago.

In 1943 I was responsible for the telephone facilities for Lord Mountbatten's SEAC HQ in the Imperial Secretariat in New Delhi. We had provided him with very expensive intercom equipment which one day gave trouble. His office was empty, I went in and crawled underneath the desk to work on a terminal strip screwed to it. I had been working for a few minutes when I heard the shuffling of feet, then a pair of splendid shoes appeared. I crawled out to the amusement of Lord Mountbatten and his assembled staff. Naturally the experience stayed in my memory but only now can I see what happened to me. By proximity he opened me up to Spirit Consciousness and set in train changes in my sympathetic nervous system which are now coming in to service for the new and improved functions. As a footnote to that story I can say that after he died he began work immediately on his great task – peace.

In the spring of 1944 I found myself under canvas for a few days on the banks of the Salween river near the town of Monywa in Burma. The river coming down from the Himalayas was broad, crystal clear with sandy banks, delicious bathing. One day two or three of us set off to visit the nearby temple, taking with us a large tin of American corned beef as a present for the Abbot. The temple complex was like a small town, very beautiful, all painted white with white doves fluttering around and the aeolian bells tinkling in the breeze. The Abbot received us in a large dim hall. He was very old and spoke to us in English as he had been to Oxford University as a young man. I cannot remember a word he said but I was vaguely aware that something very important was happening to me. The temple was on the site of a Spirit 7 healing centre, to which energy I was opened. This led to major brain changes over the subsequent forty years which enabled me to heal Soul 5 which is needed for Right Path sexual love.

My wife and I were on holiday in Rhodes in 1967 where there were two significant happenings. The first occurred when we visited the site of an ancient town which was first occupied about 6,000 years ago by the north African healers who had been invited to Rhodes to deal with an epidemic of typhus. There my level of consciousness Mind 8 was blocked. This resulted in the gift of healing glandular fever. The other happening was in Rhodes Town where I was opened to a new level of consciousness Universe 1. This gave me protection when healing cancer patients.

Shortly after the six-day war I was fortunate to be invited to Israel on business and was able to see something of that extraordinary country. Like all tourists I visited the 'wailing wall', the remains of an ancient temple. There I was opened up to Cosmic energy 6. The last time I was opened up to that energy was about 10,000 years ago. I lost it then as the result of a dis-ease, known today as spotted fever or cerebro-spinal fever. It was epidemic at the time and proved fatal to me. In subsequent incarnations I was born with a modified and inferior central nervous system which was incapable of operating the true cleansing function. Regaining that energy led to nervous system changes which gave me back that function but with protection against the disease.

In the spring of 1978 my wife and I and two friends went to the south of France to stay in an old farmhouse lent to us by a friend. When we arrived there Ronnie, one of the friends, said that the place did not feel very good so I told him to clean it up. We went from room to room uneventfully until Ronnie went into a little room under the roof and came out much shaken. What he encountered was a bad influence. Although the encounter was unpleasant to him it was paradoxically a very good influence because it was an aggregation of human levels of consciousness. They were the elements of souls of unwanted babies and old people who had been put to death in that room. Ronnie's intervention healed them of fear so they would be ready for another incarnation.

Another memorable encounter was with Dr Marcel Vogel, Chief Scientist to IBM, in the spring of 1983 at a Radionics Conference in England. He is the world authority on every form of light and has updated Einstein's theory of relativity by introducing a new factor – human consciousness. One morning I was walking along the hotel corridor when I saw him giving healing to an elderly woman. I asked if I could join in to which he assented. When he had finished I cleared a bunch of allergies after which he was able to clear some sorrow from her Mind. Afterwards we worked together for an hour or so. When we had finished he invited me to his room where he gave me one of his healing crystals. I learned afterwards that he hand shapes the crystals to tune them to the people buying them. He had made mine before we met. As I was typing that passage I was prompted to pick up and hold the crystal for a couple of minutes. As I did so I was given the gifts of healing the Sun, Cosmic and Universe Bodies and giving protection to the Whole Being. I hope I was able to help him a little physically in return.

These experiences, whilst unique to me, are not unique in their nature. I believe that thousands of people in this country have had many similar experiences but have not been aware of them. In my case I only began to be aware of them a few months ago. Many readers, with the aid of the pendulum, will be able to recall significant experiences in their lives. It is very desirable that they should do so because it will enable them, when necessary, to look back into problems their patients have had in previous incarnations and so clear blockages. I said in the introduction that there was growing in society a feeling of optimism. I believe that this is largely due to a subconscious realisation of these manifestations of Divine purpose.

Guided Tours

A notable feature of the past five years has been what I call 'guided tours': these are occasions when a friend, invariably a sensitive or a healer, and I, have been guided, either in a car or on foot to one or more locations. There is never any doubt that a 'tour' is taking place. There is a sensory 'hush' when I know that I have been taken over by a Deva. If driving we get in the car, having no idea of our destination, and allow the car to go wherever it, or rather the Deva, wishes. Sometimes there is only one stopping place, sometimes more. Favourite places for these stops are the high ground above Cheddar Gorge, and Wells Cathedral. The gorge is important because many thousands of years ago it was a university, mostly devoted to the study of healing. It is still an active Soul energy centre. The chapter-house of Wells Cathedral is a Cosmic healing and knowledge centre. It was partially reactivated, after two thousand years, when two friends and I found ourselves there during a tour in May 1979 of which I will say more later.

The first 'tour' was, I think, in the summer of 1977 when a dowsing and healing friend, Gay, and I were guided in the car to a convenient parking place near the head of the gorge. We then walked back on fairly level ground in the direction of the foot of the gorge, being directed to five different locations. At each one we paused for a few minutes without knowing the reason, the tour ending when we returned to the car. I now realise that we were being opened up to Air

Consciousness. In both of us major brain changes were being put in train which led to our respiration function being moved to the proper part of the brain from which it had been displaced 10,000 years ago. The change now enables Gay and me and many others to generate Air vitality which is needed for perceiving spirits, so that we can co-operate with them in our healing. The disease which caused the displacement was pneumonia.

Two important tours took place in May 1980 when a healing friend, Clive, together with Jan, a friend of his from the USA, paid us a visit. The first tour was preceded by a workshop with Jan apparently as the main recipient. It was an extraordinary session which went on for about two hours, during which I was guided to play a record of Schubert's Quintet in C Major in order that Franz could take part in the proceedings. Incidentally I found that Jan had bought this record at about the same time as I had purchased mine, and I subsequently discovered that my oldest friend, Tom, in Northumberland, had also bought a copy at about this time. In the event I was the main recipient of that session. I acquired Sun Consciousness which led to massive changes in the lymph system resulting later in full lymph circulation, giving proper cleansing of the lymph by the gall-bladder with the residues being disposed of by a new connection from the gall-bladder to the colon. After that indoor session we walked to the top of the Congresbury Cadbury, an ancient site on top of a low hill which is a Spirit centre. Here we were guided to ten different positions. The net result was that we each got rid of a number of redundant chakras, perceptions and levels of consciousness. The outcome for me was the start of major changes in my sympathetic nervous system for a changed sexual function. The result for Jan was his acquisition of a number of gifts, the most obvious being that of physical guidance and the ability to perceive fields and energy and healing centres.

The next morning it was a guided tour to Cheddar. I

parked the car near the top of the gorge on the right-hand side of the road and we walked back above the gorge. By this time Jan's perception of energy centres was very active and as we walked his hands waved about as he sensed positions where we had to pause, sometimes to give distant healing to someone and sometimes to receive healing from spirits. At one point a Cosmic spirit who gave his name as Uesti gave me healing and knowledge of a method of clearing environmental energy blockages by hand postures. These are quite beautiful and are clearly related to some Eastern dances. In all we visited ten positions. The objective of the walk was to open up our Air and Water Bodies to new energies. After several brain changes this led to improved protection so that we were able safely to receive the Cosmic energies needed for new and improved functions. Our tour then took us to the chapter-house of Wells Cathedral where we meditated for a few minutes. We were then escorted into the Bishop's Palace garden where the tour ended after a short time. The objective of that tour was to open us up to new Soul energies for healing people so that they could foresee 'peace'. Those gifts are now coming into operation. We also helped, unconsciously to switch on three cosmic energies.

Another Cheddar tour took place about two years ago with a friend and our dog. Ralph and I were guided to two positions; then, as we were walking back to the car, Jill moved off the path and stood about twenty yards away. We soon realised that she was showing us a spot we had not been able to sense and we walked over to her. The first two points were for perceptions 7 and 8, (perception of fields, energy centres, energies and spirits). Up to that time those perceptions had been 'lent' to me by a friend. The result was that my level of consciousness 8, (brothers and sisters for support of levels of consciousness, understanding, knowledge and perception) was cleared for its proper job. The third position which Jill sensed was a healing centre for healing the Spirit of dogs.

A very recent tour involved my publisher. I had gone to see him to discuss this book when I got the signal that a 'tour' was on. We were guided to a little church at one of the Deverills. The first place was outside and at the back of the church, after which we were led inside. The first spot was to enable him to pick up level of consciousness 9 (right path) which he had mislaid 2,000 years ago. Inside the church we both picked up level 10 (future) so that we and others could foresee the spread of the gift of unconditional love. We had lost that level at the time Mary was born.

Two years ago a woman came to see me from London. I had come to her attention because of an article I had written, but she did not say why she had come. The first afternoon I gave her some healing, I still do not know what for, and the next morning was a 'tour' to the chapter-house at Wells where we meditated. When we were walking away from the cathedral I experienced a strange sensation involving all my muscles. The objective of the visit to the cathedral was so that she could give me proximity healing to bring the control of my Sun Body into the correct part of the brain. The strange sensation that followed was as a result of the change taking place. That manoeuvre subsequently allowed my healing function to move to the correct part of the brain thus increasing my healing powers. Overall she benefited by the acquisition of levels 9 and 10 (right path and future).

Glastonbury,
The Chalice Well and The Blue Bowl
and The Shroud of Turin

In March of 1984 a French woman came to stay with neigh-
bours for a few days. As soon as I saw her I knew that I had
been in touch with her for the past three years and that she
was my Air sister. One day I took Françoise and my neigh-
bours to Wells to see the Cathedral and to Glastonbury
where we visited the Abbey ruins and the Chalice Well. The
well-shaft is thought to have been constructed in the twelfth
century but in fact the well has been a healing site for several
thousand years. In the eighteenth century thousands of
people visited it and many cures were recorded. The Chalice
Well handbook states that the fashion, or the faith, gradually
declined but that healings have continued to the present
day. The well is an Air and Sun centre (the Abbey is the Soul
Centre of the earth), and at the time of its great popularity it
was emitting, and the water contained, Air and Sun energies, 5, 6, 7, 8, 9 and 10. At the end of the eighteenth century
only energies 9 and 10 remained. During our visit emission
of a further sixteen energies began, that is the full range for
Air and Sun. It is about 2,000 years since the site was so
active. Needless to say, if a sample were submitted to
chemical analysis the opinion would be that it was only
chalybeate water. This stupid reliance on chemical analysis
is the main reason why our spas have declined in number

and in usage. Many of them are very powerful and a lot of people with chronic ailments could benefit by visiting the right ones.

Two years before when I had visited the well in a party led by Paul Soloman we were shown, but not allowed to touch, a beautiful blue bowl which we were told had an amazing history. I sensed that it had great power but I made no attempt to analyse it. On this second occasion it was not possible for us to see it. The bowl had been discovered in an extraordinary manner by Wellesley Tudor Pole who subsequently founded the Chalice Well Trust. In a little book, *Wellesley Tudor Pole, Appreciation and Evaluation* by Oliver C. Villiers there is an account of the remarkable history of the bowl from its discovery in 1906 to the present day. Tudor Pole immediately knew that it had remarkable and unique properties. He said that "ever since its recovery at Avalon in 1906, this blue sapphire bowl has spent its life alternately between unseen realms (apparently asleep in an external sense) – and sleeping above whilst intensively active and awake below." Its significance to him can be judged by the fact that he took it with him on many journeys in this country and abroad. I should mention here that until his death in 1968 Tudor Pole had been one of the leading sensitives in the world.

The following brief account of the earlier history of the bowl and its purpose is now being given to me by Tudor Pole who says he wants me to include this section about the well and the bowl in this book. The bowl was made in Syria in AD 10, having been commissioned by a Roman. In AD 20 he presented it to Christ whom he greatly admired. It was used at the last supper and after the crucifixion passed into the hands of Peter who took it to Rome. It remained there until 430 when for safe keeping it was taken to Verona. In 810 St Cuthbert took it to Glastonbury and buried it in the field near Brides Hill where it was found. The bowl is possessed by spirits Universe 7, 8, 9 and 10 and is presently dispensing world-wide the gift of true healing to many healers. The last time this gift was widely available was long before the last fall to which I referred earlier. A healer is practising true healing when he knows that the cause of all dis-ease is the presence of discarnates in the being, and he is able to clear only those which should be cleared because many possessions are helpful. It is by possessing levels of consciousness that our family, friends, fellow-workers and brothers and sisters are able to help us when we are in great need.

Shortly after typing the above passage I read an article in *The Readers Digest* which described a massive investigation of the Shroud of Turin by many scientists over a period of three years. They found nothing that would preclude the shroud's being authentic but they did find massive evidence that it could have been. Obviously no scientific investigation could prove that it was. However, Tudor Pole told me a little later that it was in fact authentic and that the same day we were visiting the Chalice Well the shroud began to dispense to healers world-wide the gift of protection for levels of consciousness and perception against bad influences and psychic aggression. This means that for the first time for many thousands of years it will be possible for many healers quickly to acquire more healing, cleansing and protective powers which will enable them to cleanse people and animals, and the environment generally of bad influences and widen the range of dis-ease they can clear.

Two months after I wrote about the bowl a friend lent me *A Man Seen from Afar* by Wellesley Tudor Pole and Rosamund Lehmann published by Neville Spearman in 1965 in which Tudor Pole relates some of his memories of the life and times of Jesus. In one chapter, The Upper Room, he describes in detail the room in which the last supper was held. On the table was a cup which he describes as 'a shallow saucer-like cup made of glass, multi-coloured yet silvery hued and of fine and semi-transparent design' from which he says the disciples drank sacramentally, one by one. A little further on Rosamund Lehmann says, "I questioned W.T.P. about the multi-coloured cup or bowl of glass so vividly described. It would seem from what he told me to have had a tangled history, both factual and esoteric. This vessel or its exact replica still exists and is known to have been the subject of numerous conflicting opinions and conjectures. One day perhaps the truth about it will be brought to light, but apparently the time is not yet ripe. Meanwhile it is in safe keeping."

In another chapter Rosamund Lehmann tells how she wrote to Tudor Pole about apparent contradictions in the four New Testament versions of the life of Jesus. She quoted one passage which she said seemed to be in the nature of a clue, cryptically, deliberately planted, pointing to an event of the utmost significance in the drama. "And there followed him a certain young man, having a linen cloth about his naked body; and the young man laid hold on him. And he left the linen cloth and fled from them naked.' (*Mark* XIV 51-52.) Some weeks later Tudor Pole replied, "Your young man was virile, and possessed a particular kind of magnetism with which the linen robe he wore had become imbued. It was this linen cloth that was used to provide the etheric double whilst Jesus was in the tomb. In fact it was the major portion of the cerements. Now, nothing happens 'by accident'; the details of all cosmic events affecting human destiny are prepared for centuries before they take place outwardly. When he touched Jesus your young man had a sudden overwhelming vision of the horrors of the approaching tragedy – more than he could stand. Casting off the garment he fled, not even knowing of the service he had been destined to render Jesus."

I also believe that Cosmic and Universe events are predestined and the fact that knowledge of the bowl and the shroud are becoming widely known, as is something of their significance and function, is a strong indication of forthcoming events on earth which will change the course of mankind and indeed of all life on earth.

Final Stages

It is only now, seven years after my loss of protection, that I have a fairly good idea what happened. The condition was caused by psychic aggression and doses of uranium and curare. I was stripped of most of my natural protection and many of my perceptions and levels of consciousness. I survived because thirty friends came to my aid by occupying levels of consciousness and perceptions. A case of benevolent possession! The other side of the coin was that thirty levels came in, some of them for the first time for many thousands of years. From a healing point of view my Earth, Nature and Soul Bodies were knocked out but five new ones came in, Air, Water, Sun, Mind and Cosmic. My Universe Body which came in as soon as I began to heal survived intact. Two big bonuses were that my perception 8 opened up so that I was able to get help from spirits and my level of consciousness 4 opened up so that I was able initially to get help from five fellow-workers but now I have many. I rarely have to find a helper consciously. In the case of the man who was told that his leg would have to be amputated I got help from forty humans, eight spirits and two animals. The greatest gift I received in the new phase was the ability to clear, by touch, Mind blockages, caused mainly by a guilty conscience. My greatest helper was my wife, Isobel, who resolutely protected all the thirty people who came to my aid.

In recent months as my Being has been under renewal it

has been fascinating and thrilling to observe my brothers
and sisters and fellow-workers taking up their proper positions in my Being and thus clearing levels of consciousness
and perceptions in preparation for the commissioning of the
improved systems and functions. About six months ago for
a while I had consciously to help my patients to find their
brothers and sisters, but this is now an unconscious process,
as is helping them to find their fellow-workers.

On Good Friday morning 1984 I was told that from the
time of my critical illness when I was seven I had been under
the protection of two Jesuits, one from 1923 until his death
in 1964 and the other from 1965. The protection was unavailable for one year during which time aggression started
brain changes which led to a changed cardio-vascular circulation system which was needed to harmonise with the new
circulating lymph system twenty years later. In the afternoon of that day together with two friends I went for a walk
on the Congresbury Cadbury. As we walked along, my
friends, fairly new to dowsing and healing, were dowsing
and I was confirming their findings; numerous energies for
birds, various animals and human beings. In all we noted
thirty. This was a clear indication that their perception 7
(fields, energy centres and energies) was working well. Our
first stop on this guided tour was at an Air centre where five
new energies appeared, 6, 7, 8, 9 and 10. They last appeared
there 6,000 years ago. We were then guided to a site where
there were some large stones, the remains of a covered
structure built 8,000 years ago by the Druids or their ante-
cedents. It was a fertility centre for humans, animals, plants
and trees. Here we sat down for a few minutes whilst brain
changes were put in train for the gifts of meditation, kundalini and right sexuality, that is when the last element of
Self has gone and God is in charge, as in everything else.
Whilst we were there nine new energies appeared, Nature 5
and 6, Mind 5 and 6, Soul 7, Cosmic 1 and 2 and Universe 9
and 10. The site had been in use off and on until the arrival

of the Romans who liquidated the Druids by black magic as they had earlier liquidated the Essenes. The disease was leukaemia. Some people today have the same black magic gift.

On the Monday morning I was told that, simultaneous with many thousands of people getting Cosmic Consciousness, the dismantling of the major aggressive networks would begin because they had served their purpose, and the operators in the networks would find that the protection afforded them by their organisations would be withdrawn, thus leaving them in a similar situation to many of their victims. Very many of them will need healing. I hope there are not many healers about like a man and wife I heard of recently who will not help atheists. The main character defect of psychic aggressors is their desire to exercise power over their fellow-men. Perhaps this is what Christ meant when he said "The meek shall inherit the earth"! I was aware of two major happenings that day. Cosmic energies 3, 5 and 8 began to emanate from the Great Pyramid and radioactive metals began to decay rapidly to provide the chakras needed by all forms of life for the new functions and gifts.

Since Easter 1985 a huge cleansing operation has been in progress, cleansing thousands of people of bad influences, the products of psychic aggression, toxins and disease residues. The cleansing is being done by many people whose cleansing function is working fully. It is being achieved by proximity, at a distance and by contact. The vast majority of those doing the cleansing are unaware of the fact. I have been able to observe measles, mumps and other disease residues, bad influences and the products of psychic aggression being cleared from my body. This has enabled some important levels to come into service, Spirit levels for systemic change, Cosmic levels for the improved functions and Universe levels for new gifts. I know that similar things are happening to many other people.

In the summer of 1984 I was prompted to pick up and

read a section of Dr Guirdham's book *The Lake and the Castle* which like some of his other books deals with the experiences of a number of people who have met in this and other lives. His group had been on my mind for some years because in all his books I have read there is an undercurrent of unhappiness and pessimism. They seem to be trapped in a cycle of black magic. I was told by Sai Baba that this was so because as a group about 10,000 years ago they had been subjected to a black magic attack which had caused them to exchange elements of their beings with the earth, plants, trees and animals. This resulted in their losing a number of gifts which had aroused the envy of the people amongst whom they lived. Today they are regaining the gifts they lost. Although on the face of it the original attack had been made because of feelings of envy, in fact the aggressors had no choice. The real cause was the decision of the Universe Spirit that we should learn technology. As this phase slows down, mankind is being given gifts which will enable us to live more in harmony with our environment and thus be happier.

At the beginning of July of that year I went for a two weeks holiday to Kefalonia where a number of important events occurred. The first was the sighting of a golden eagle. On a trip to the north of the island we had stopped at a point about 1,500 feet above the sea and looking down 500 feet below we saw a golden eagle slowly spiralling up on a thermal. We were able to watch the bird for about ten minutes and for a while it was only about forty yards from us. The whole party was very much moved and excited by the experience. The eagle is now a fellow-worker of mine. His strong line is spirit. Another day I went with a coach-party to Olympia on the Greek mainland which is the main protection centre of the world. Whilst we were there ten new energies appeared, level 10 of all the bodies. It is 10,000 years since these energies were last present at Olympia. Two other important events were my meeting two young women, Susanne, a young Danish woman presently teaching in Greenland who is my Universe 10 sister and fellow-worker, and Christly, a young Dutch woman who is my Cosmic 10 sister and fellow-worker.

In the October I was twice admitted to hospital for treatment following psychic attacks. Each time the target was my Air Body whose protection at the time was poor because of systemic changes taking place. On the first occasion the real objective at Universe level was to clear a miasm from my level Air 2 which I had had since contracting bubonic plague 200 years ago. On the second occasion two miasms were cleared, Soul 1 which I had had since the Romans attacked the Druids and Sun 8 which I had had since an attack of black death 300 years ago. Clearance of these miasms enabled me to cure rheumatism, thrombosis and water retention. It is noteworthy that all the occupants of the three wards I was in had all been the targets of psychic attack. We were all given tablets which protected us from psychic attack. If members of the medical profession are aware of the use of psychic attack it is a pity that they do not admit it. This may prompt some sufferers to contact healers with the object of getting their protection function working rather than continuing to take drugs for the rest of their lives.

All the major aggressive networks are being dismantled and the organising spirits of the networks are taking up their proper positions as levels of consciousness for the Cosmic and Universe Bodies of many men and women. My physical constitution and that of many others has changed to a superior arrangement as has that of many animals. At the same time the earth is being cleansed of human and animal elements which have been present since humans and animals lost them as a result of disease.

Throughout the six years massive physical works were proceeding, new arteries for brain, organs and muscles and additional ducts for the improved systems and thousands of nerves. Probably the most important changes took place in the brain. Before the change eight functions were controlled by the left-hand side of the brain and two by the right. Now five functions are being controlled by the left-hand side and the five non-physical by the right. Gifts are controlled by the front of the brain. I have had this arrangement before but it was a long time ago. It is interesting to speculate what God has been using the right-hand side and most of the front of the brain for all that time. Gifts of course are the means whereby we are able to perform complex functions without conscious effort. That is when God is in the driving-seat.

Available to us are countless gifts but the standard issue as the Universe levels come into service are:

1 Physical well-being
2 Harmony with the environment
3 Comforting
4 Physical guidance (including muscular co-ordination)
5 Sexual love
6 Peace of mind and meditation
7 Unconditional love, true healing
8 Lightheartedness
9 Helping people to get the right guidance
10 Knowledge of the future

Conclusion

It is inevitable in a book such as this, when my perceptions and consciousness have been changing from one day to another that there will be errors and misconceptions, but any present will be of little consequence because I know the model is adequate and substantially correct as I have been using it successfully over the past four years. Most important of all however, I, at the age of sixty-eight, and friends and patients and some dogs are enjoying a superior constitution, and I am also enjoying the Universe gifts and many others. My dependence on nicotine and alcohol has greatly diminished.

After the change in my Being seven years ago I began increasingly to experience the phenomenon of synchronicity but now synchronistic events are the norm; in fact my life is one long train of synchronicity as I pursue my course along the right path. Things are now properly arranged. If I have a decision to make involving someone else there is no discussion until our spirits have met and discussed the problem in the noumenal world where we have the benefit of advice from our friends and fellow-workers. Apart from the superior healing powers and gifts I now have, the change in my ordinary daily life is astonishing. Although I do not know what each day will bring I am certain that it will be full and purposeful. There are no periods when I do not know what to do. In the course of working sessions, frequently guidance comes along on day to day matters. I do not have to ask for the help or guidance, it just comes along – when to change my car, when to buy a new carpet or curtains. Each day starts with a number of events planned, but they are concealed and step by step as the day progresses I uncover them.

Now that the interactions between myself and my thirty friends have finished the garden too is in splendid form. All the flowers and vegetables are doing well and I had the finest crops of tomatoes I have ever had. Seven years ago only three main energies were getting through to the earth and the plants, Water, Soul and Cosmic, together with thirty sub-energies, but today ten main energies and ninety sub-energies are getting through. No artificial fertilisers are needed. This improvement has come about as a result of the clearance of numerous miasms and bad influences. As I have been able to perceive weeds I have been able without conscious effort to ask them to go away and they have done so. It is not only doctors and nutritionists who need to accept this concept of environmental energies. Farmers and agriculturists need to do so as well.

I can see now that the last events to take place before the systems, improved functions, and gifts could come into service were the cleansing of miasms, innoculation residues, poisons, antibiotics, black magic and witchcraft from my body. All had impaired proper functioning in some way, particularly the non-physical functions. Four innoculation residues were cleared; smallpox which had impaired my cleansing function, cholera which had impaired my protective function, yellow fever which had impaired my healing function and tetanus which had impaired my energising function. Antibiotics had impaired my elimination function. Thus innoculations and vaccination give us protection from acute disease at the expense of our higher functions. This explains why our environment has become increasingly 'dirty' in the past sixty years. Readers, if they wish, and have the necessary sensitivity will be able to examine the harmful effects of other innoculations such as measles and whooping-cough. The contraceptive pill incidentally impairs the protection against psychic aggression.

I find I have been given doses of poison, sometimes cocktails, on twenty different occasions by seven different agencies: all except arsenic and aluminium in homoeopathic form. The first poison I was given was aluminium by a fellow-officer in Barrackpore in India in 1944 who I think would have described himself as a committed Christian. They seem to be a particularly virulent, fanatical and intolerant type of person. Readers with Universe Consciousness and a good perception 5 will be able to detect some or all of these poisons. It is no good expecting doctors to find them, they are unaware of all this. This type of poisoning has been going on at an increasing rate for the past forty-five years. Thirty per cent of the adult population is affected in some degree. They go to see the doctor and are given another poison. Fortunately this state of affairs is coming to an end and with the new energies becoming available cleansing will improve the non-physical functions.

I can now see a particularly horrible misuse of powers, Mind control. In hypnosis the hypnotist gains access to level 6 of the Mind, which in most people is normally blocked, and implants beneficial instructions or suggestions. In Mind control the operator gets distant access to Mind level 6 of his victim and tells him what to do. In this way people can be made to do things which are quite out of character. Even if the target's Soul is strong enough to resist the instructions, a state of mental confusion is created. Mind control has been extensively used by many organisations in the past thirty years. A similar form of attack is where reason is blocked. This is achieved by blocking level 6 of the Soul.

The reasons for the organised psychic aggression we have witnessed over the past forty-six years are various. Some national networks whose aims are often the subversion of whole populations are directed at sensitives who have the gifts to obstruct them. The Church seems to have an implacable hostility towards healers. It seems that the Masons have some ancient knowledge which they want to keep to themselves. There are some bodies who seek to capture the Minds and Souls of the dead and the living. Then there are local covens in which many participate for what they think is harmless fun, little knowing that a lot of them are being used for base purposes. But whatever the motives of the aggressors it is a remarkable and wonderful fact that at Universe level each and every one of them has a job to do and they are divinely guided to do it. But now that the aggressive networks have been dismantled and healers have new powers, fear is being dispelled from the Beings of millions of people. When fear goes out love comes in and with it come gifts. So here we have a massive demonstration of the fact that no matter how aggressive, prejudiced and dogmatic we are, in the major Cosmic and Universe issues we are made, by the spirit world, to do that which will lead to the right outcome. The message then is simple; let us cooperate with the spirit world so that our individual paths harmonise with the Divine trends which will somehow be fulfilled whether we cooperate or not. We have to learn how to get proper guidance from higher intelligences. The one thing that can prevent us from getting right guidance is pride.

The one thing necessary to be able to do useful work is acceptance of the fact that there is a noumenal world whose occupants have great responsibilities and power and are anxious to help us. For that they need our recognition and cooperation. The problems facing mankind, if we dared to look at them, must seem insurmountable and indeed they will be if we carry on in the present fashion. But I am sure that just as individuals can find the Right Path, so can nations and the world as a whole. Our great malaise is manifest in the increasing number of nonsenses around. There is increasing attention to 'needs' and less to 'obligations'. If matters go wrong the 'in' thing today is to find someone else to carry the can.

People who hold strong religious beliefs and want to learn to heal will have difficulty with holistic healing because most religions are based on convention, prejudice and dogma and depend on the written word, no matter how long ago it was written, nor how expurgated it is, whereas the approach described in this book is based on seeking the right path by asking for help from those individuals, operating in other dimensions, who are qualified to give it. For everyone wanting to heal in the way outlined here there is a guru waiting. Readers should not feel from the above that I am knocking the Church, far from it. As is the case with all institutions, in the history of the Church there must be much it is not proud of, nevertheless it has given protection and comfort to countless numbers of people at the price of restricted awareness. Who is to say that its role in the past 1,600 years has been wrong? Now however, the Church has a golden opportunity with its thousands of priests to assume its proper role, healing. And that means healing anyone who comes for help regardless of religious beliefs. If the church does not take this opportunity it may well wither away.

There is no doubt that we are at a turning-point in the history of the world. With expanded consciousness being acquired by more and more people we will have a greater respect for, and understanding of, each other and of the animal kingdom, plants and the earth. As level of consciousness 4 (fellow-workers) comes in so people will get increasing help over the air in whatever right endeavour they are engaged. Politicians and people in positions of power and authority will benefit greatly in this way because at present many of them are very lonely. So the formulation of policies for businesses and governments will increasingly be influenced by the heightened consciousness of the general public and democracy will take a giant step forward. For

the individual however the biggest prize will be the acquisition of Right Path Consciousness and thus of Divine
guidance.

As the consciousness of people expands and with it respect for everything, so our need for convention will reduce.
People will not do things in a certain way simply because
convention requires it. With their expanded awareness they
will see every situation as unique, requiring a specific decision or action. In the realm of sexuality the weakening of
convention will be increasingly apparent. There will be a
great increase in sexual powers for older people, and as
jealousy and fear go there will increasingly be sexual love
outside marriage. But this will not be irresponsible because
on right path it will only take place with the Spirit agree-
ment of all those concerned. The marriage vows, which
forty per cent of married people break at some time or
another, will be seen as an attempt by the Church to ensure
that if we do break the vows we will be troubled by a guilty
conscience. Sexual love for many people will become a
much more intense and beautiful experience having an
important role in cleansing our Beings. Increasingly sexual
love will be accompanied by the experience of Kundalini
which is a state of bliss where only Spirit consciousness
remains.

If I had had the stamina and the time I could have written a
massive tome rather than a little book but that would have
defeated the object of the exercise. This book is not to be
read and put away; it is a basis for work. As the author of
this book it may seem an odd thing to say but for this type of
work I am against books. For the three-dimensional life we
have to have books and the conventional methods of learning are necessary, but for this subject the real teachers can
only be occupants of the noumenal world. Progress and
benefits will only follow from right work whatever that
may be. Although simple dowsing can be of great help to

anyone for healing and in day to day life, for those who have the time and inclination, advanced dowsing for guidance is the way to a new and more positive life wherein adventures of the spirit come in increasing numbers as new break-throughs are achieved. This way of working will soon show how inadequate is the materialistic and superficial way of thinking for the massive problems facing us. To any sensitive the idea that the world's problems can be solved by examining them one by one without the help of the nou-menal world, is absurd. Dutch-elm disease, a man-made disease, is a case in point. Another is the problem of acid rain. No one is going to get the answers to these problems by peering into a microscope and using a massive computer.

For any reader who has followed my arguments, the limitations of the conventional medical approach should be obvious. Doctors disregard our etheric bodies which are the source of our conscience, beliefs, emotions and ambitions. They have no knowledge of the vitalities or of the connective tissues which are so important for our well-being. Do they even know the ten main human functions and have they any knowledge of the perceptions and levels of consciousness? Has any doctor ever said "I am afraid your urinary system is inefficient because it is being controlled by the wrong part of the brain, but I can recommend a herbal remedy which will enable you to be healthier than you are now?" Doctors, by medical tests can only identify about five per cent of the allergies which trouble us. If they could dowse they would probably pick up between thirty and sixty per cent. Why have they virtually thrown out herbal based remedies and increasingly relied on complex expensive and noxious chemical compounds all of which sooner or later have serious side-effects. I understand that the British Medical Association after pressure from Prince Charles has launched an investigation into complementary medicine. It is obvious that as a body they are as completely incompetent for the job as would be a panel of parsons. I further understand that the EEC have healing in their sights. God forbid! Healing support for doctors will not come about as a result of establishment decisions: it will happen gradually and naturally as the consciousness of the general public and doctors expands.

Work Sheets

PROBLEM AREAS

Allergies

Diet

Miasms

Bad influences

Family

Pets

Poisons, e.g. lead, aluminium, copper

Underground streams or water

Subsoil

Cosmetics and toilet preparations

Other

OTHER THERAPIES

Doctor

Chiropractor

Homoeopath

Herbalist

Physiotherapist

Another healer

Osteopath

Radionic practitioner

Acupuncturist

A visit to another place

Other

FOODS TO IMPROVE FUNCTIONING

Energy Generation and Distribution – Wholemeal bread, meat, liver, salt, pepper, spices

Sensory and Nervous – Fish, honey, mushrooms

Elimination – Milk, prunes, rye, figs, eggs, chocolate

Muscular Activity and Coordination – Cheese, sunflower seeds, honey

Sexual – Greens, fruit, salads, butter, tea, coffee

Thinking – Honey, citrus fruits, caraway seeds

Healing – Honey, cheese, citrus fruits

Cleansing – Legumes, leeks, caraway seeds

Energising – Honey, sugar, onions, cheese

Protection – Yoghourt, nuts, garlic, molasses, beer

NUTRITIONAL SUPPLEMENTS, REMEDIES AND SKIN PREPARATIONS

The following are those most commonly needed

Bach Rescue Remedy and cream

Oil of Sandalwood

Betula ointment

Pakua

Brewers Yeast

Pulsatilla Compound tablets

Feverfew tablets

Rose Hip tablets

Garlic Perles

Rosemary infusions and soap

Honey

Rutin Compound tablets

Kelp

Vita Florem

Oil of Olbas

These may also be needed

Black Willow Compound tablets

Juna beans

Calendula ointment

Lecithin

Cider Vinegar capsules

Marshmallow root

Comfrey ointment and tablets

Saffron Oil Seed capsules

Cranesbill Compound tablets

Spirulina

Echinacea tablets

Wheat Germ oil

Ginseng tablets

Witchazel cream

Gravel Root Compound tablets

PRINCIPAL SOURCES OF VITAMINS

Vitamin A should be produced by the Earth Body: Halibut-liver oil, egg yolk, carrots.

Vitamin B should be produced by the Air Body: Brewers yeast, eggs, yoghourt, whole rice, sunflower seeds, tea, coffee.

Vitamin B12 should be produced by the Water Body: Legumes, parsley, chicory, curry, milk, coffee, tea, wholemeal bread.

Vitamin C should be produced by the Sun Body: Sprouted shoots, legumes, green and red peppers, citrus fruits, tea, coffee.

Vitamin D should be produced by the Spirit Body: Animal fats, liver, egg yolk, oysters, beer, wholemeal bread.

Vitamin E should be produced by the Universe Body: Wheat germ oil, sprouted seeds and grain, whisky.

Vitamin F should be produced by the Soul Body: Polyunsaturated oils, butter, beer, whisky and certain other spirits, coffee, tea, wholemeal bread.

Vitamin K should be produced by the Nature Body: Liver, herbs, leafy vegetables, raw cauliflower, tomatoes, coffee, tea, beer, wholemeal bread.

Vitamin P should be produced by the Cosmic Body: Rinds of citrus fruit, root ginger, horseradish, grapefruit, mixed herbs, beer, butter.

Vitamix X should be produced by the Mind Body: Brewers yeast, wheatgerm oil, liver, chives, kidneys, onion, meat, beer, whisky and certain other spirits.

HEALING TECHNIQUES

Thought	Acupressure
Meditation	Thought, whilst allowing pendulum to move
Contact (hands and fingers)	
No contact (hands and fingers)	Proximity
Visualisation	Prayer
Colour	Other

A METHOD OF DISTANT HEALING

Find
a) Problem level of Consciousness
b) Problem Body
c) Problem Chakra
Heal Chakra
Repeat above as necessary.
For miasms find which Subtle Bodies they relate to and clear them.
For bad influences, find which level of consciousness they relate to and clear them.
For poisons, find appropriate herbal remedies.
For underground water or subsoil patient should take a course of Bach Rescue Remedy until protection is adequate.
Advise on diet, remedies, nutritional supplements etc. This together with the healing should eliminate many allergies.
For other members of family and pets treat as above.
Finally ask "Have I been sufficiently diligent and imaginative?" If not, continue working.

SUGGESTED ROUTINE FOR HAND HEALING SESSION

At start of session give oral dose of Bach Rescue Remedy.
Give hand healing to both shoulders for at least five minutes or as long as necessary.
Give further hand or touch healing. Placing of hands and fingers and duration as indicated by pendulum.
At close give another dose of Rescue Remedy.
Check diet.
Check for remedies etc.
Check progress.
   Peace of mind
   Sense of well being
   Vitality
   Pain
   Changes in Bodies, Chakras and levels of Consciousness
Check for another therapy.
Fix date and time for next session if necessary.

POINTS OF ENTRY FOR CONSCIOUSNESS OF ENVIRONMENT

These may be cleared at the right time by finger touch healing.

EARTH	Finger and toe nails
AIR	First phalange of fingers and thumbs
WATER	Second phalange of fingers and thumbs
SUN	Third phalange of fingers and thumbs
NATURE	Front wrist
MIND	Back-base of ears
SOUL	Centre upper chest
SPIRIT	Shoulders
COSMIC	Back of neck
UNIVERSE	Top of head

POINTS OF ENTRY FOR SENSORY HEALING DATA

These may be cleared at the right time by thumb touch healing.

Palms of both hands	Mid-lower back
Both hands at junction of first finger	Upper chest
	Base of rib cage
Front of forearms	Shoulders
Front of upper arms	Sides of head
Upper thighs	

EXIT POINTS FOR PROXIMITY AND DISTANT HEALING ENERGIES

Thumb and finger tips	Upper temples
Edge of finger nails	Front neck
Edge of toe nails	Upper back head
Pharynx	Mid spine
Back-base of ears	Sides of head

POINTS OF ENTRY FOR MAIN ENVIRONMENTAL ENERGIES

They may be cleared at the right time by touch healing.

EARTH	Legs and feet
AIR	Chest
WATER	Lower abdomen
SUN	Arms and hands
NATURE	Buttocks
MIND	Mid back
SOUL	Shoulder blades
SPIRIT	Upper chest
COSMIC	Shoulder
UNIVERSE	Head

HAND HEALING FOR THE WHOLE BEING

Both hands to head

Both hands to shoulder blades

Both hands to chest

Both hands to lower abdomen

Both hands to mid back

Both hands to lower back

Both hands to buttocks

Both hands to front mid thighs

Both hands to back mid thighs

Both hands to calves

Both hands to base of spine

HAND HEALING TO EASE MENTAL CONFUSION

This may be done at the right time by contact with the side of the hand.

Left cheek	Right mid-abdomen
Right cheek	Inner side left shoulder blade
Front left armpit	Inner side right shoulder blade
Front right armpit	Just below left hip
Left mid-abdomen	Just below right hip

HAND HEALING TO EASE OR STOP PAIN

This may be done at the right time by contact with the ball of the thumb.

Upper back head	Left hip
Upper left chest	Right hip
Upper right chest	Outer left leg above knee
Left mid-side	Outer right leg above knee
Right mid-side	Base of spine

HAND HEALING FOR REPAIR OF THE VITAL ORGANS

These may be repaired at the right time by hand healing using both hands.

Stomach	Kidneys
Lungs	Heart
Bowel	Pancreas
Spleen	Liver
Gall bladder	Brain

HAND HEALING FOR FUNCTIONS

F1   From top of head to base of spine. Contact with base of four
       fingers. Lengthy contact may be necessary at several points.

F2   With little finger touch from top of ear round back of neck to top of
       other ear

F3   Both hands just above knee

F4   Both hands to calves

F5   Both hands to kidneys

F6   Both hands to sides of head

F7   Back of both hands applied to palms of hands

F8   Fingers applied across back of fingers of both hands

F9   Knuckles of both hands applied to knuckles of both hands

F10   Both hands to shoulders

Use of the Following Tables

The following tables can be used by a healer who has Cosmic Consciousness or who has a fellow-worker with Cosmic Consciousness. It is possible by their use to clear mental, psychological and emotional problems, caused by shock, stress and frustration, which are not amenable to conventional medicine. The problems are caused in two main ways: as a result of picking up bad influences or being subject to psychic aggression, or when the Being is moving towards superior functioning and is blocked by redundant elements. Clearance of these adverse conditions will always increase happiness and promote better physical functioning.

Method
If guided by the pendulum to the Index of Work Sheets, dowse the appropriate sheet. Then dowse down each column to find the path which will end at two vital organs. This means that a subtle energy is blocked at the first organ thus diverting the energy wrongly to the second organ. Healing is achieved when the three energies, love, light and life force, are cleared to pass through the first organ. This can be done in a number of ways, by direct request, through a fellow-worker working through you, by touch or hand healing or by the use of remedies. If these methods are ineffective you will have to resort to 'what shall I do now?' The fact that you have been guided to a particular sheet means that it is within your ability, somehow, to clear the problem.

PROBLEMS CAUSED BY SUPPRESSED EMOTIONS

Body	Chakra	Level of Understanding	Function	Corresponding Organ
1	1	1	1	Stomach
2	2	2	2	Lungs
3	3	3	3	Bowel
4	4	4	4	Spleen
5	5	5	5	Gall Bladder
6	6	6	6	Kidneys
7	7	7	7	Heart
8	8	8	8	Pancreas
9	9	9	9	Liver
10	10	10	10	Brain

PROBLEMS CAUSED BY POOR METABOLISM

Body	Chakra	Vital Organ	Function	Corresponding Organ
1	1	Brain	1	Stomach
2	2	Liver	2	Lungs
3	3	Pancreas	3	Bowel
4	4	Heart	4	Spleen
5	5	Kidneys	5	Gall Bladder
6	6	Gall Bladder	6	Kidneys
7	7	Spleen	7	Heart
8	8	Bowel	8	Pancreas
9	9	Lungs	9	Liver
10	10	Stomach	10	Brain

PROBLEMS CAUSED BY UNDERGROUND WATER AND SUBSOIL

Body	Chakra	Level of Under- standing	Level of Perception	Function	Corresponding Organ
1	1	1	1	1	Stomach
2	2	2	2	2	Lungs
3	3	3	3	3	Bowel
4	4	4	4	4	Spleen
5	5	5	5	5	Gall Bladder
6	6	6	6	6	Kidneys
7	7	7	7	7	Heart
8	8	8	8	8	Pancreas
9	9	9	9	9	Liver
10	10	10	10	10	Brain

PROBLEMS CAUSED BY ENERGY CENTRES

Body	Chakra	Level of Perception	Level of Knowledge	Level of Consciousness	Function	Corresponding Organ
1	1	1	1	1	1	Stomach
2	2	2	2	2	2	Lungs
3	3	3	3	3	3	Bowel
4	4	4	4	4	4	Spleen
5	5	5	5	5	5	Gall Bladder
6	6	6	6	6	6	Kidneys
7	7	7	7	7	7	Heart
8	8	8	8	8	8	Pancreas
9	9	9	9	9	9	Liver
10	10	10	10	10	10	Brain

PROBLEMS CAUSED BY DISEASE RESIDUES

Body	Chakra	Level of Conscious-ness	Level of Perception	Function	Corresponding Organ
1	1	1	1	1	Stomach
2	2	2	2	2	Lungs
3	3	3	3	3	Bowel
4	4	4	4	4	Spleen
5	5	5	5	5	Gall Bladder
6	6	6	6	6	Kidneys
7	7	7	7	7	Heart
8	8	8	8	8	Pancreas
9	9	9	9	9	Liver
10	10	10	10	10	Brain

PROBLEMS CAUSED BY TOXINS

Body	Level of Conscious-ness	Level of Perception	Chakra	Function	Corresponding Organ
1	1	1	1	1	Stomach
2	2	2	2	2	Lungs
3	3	3	3	3	Bowel
4	4	4	4	4	Spleen
5	5	5	5	5	Gall Bladder
6	6	6	6	6	Kidneys
7	7	7	7	7	Heart
8	8	8	8	8	Pancreas
9	9	9	9	9	Liver
10	10	10	10	10	Brain

PROBLEMS CAUSED BY SHOCK

Body	Chakra	Level of Consciousness	Function	Corresponding Organ
1	1	1	1	Stomach
2	2	2	2	Lungs
3	3	3	3	Bowel
4	4	4	4	Spleen
5	5	5	5	Gall Bladder
6	6	6	6	Kidneys
7	7	7	7	Heart
8	8	8	8	Pancreas
9	9	9	9	Liver
10	10	10	10	Brain

ALLERGIES

Redundant Levels of Perception	Function	Corresponding Organ
1	1	Stomach
2	2	Lungs
3	3	Bowel
4	4	Spleen
5	5	Gall Bladder
6	6	Kidneys
7	7	Heart
8	8	Pancreas
9	9	Liver
10	10	Brain

ADDICTIONS

Redundant Bodies	Chakra	Function	Corresponding Organ
1	1	1	Stomach
2	2	2	Lungs
3	3	3	Bowel
4	4	4	Spleen
5	5	5	Gall Bladder
6	6	6	Kidneys
7	7	7	Heart
8	8	8	Pancreas
9	9	9	Liver
10	10	10	Brain

PROBLEMS CAUSED BY STRESS

Level of Perception	Function	Corresponding Organ
1	1	Stomach
2	2	Lungs
3	3	Bowel
4	4	Spleen
5	5	Gall Bladder
6	6	Kidneys
7	7	Heart
8	8	Pancreas
9	9	Liver
10	10	Brain

PHOBIAS

Redundant Element of Body	Level of Consciousness	Function	Corresponding Organ
1	1	1	Stomach
2	2	2	Lungs
3	3	3	Bowel
4	4	4	Spleen
5	5	5	Gall Bladder
6	6	6	Kidneys
7	7	7	Heart
8	8	8	Pancreas
9	9	9	Liver
10	10	10	Brain

PROBLEMS CAUSED BY FRUSTRATION

Body	Chakra	Level of Knowledge	Function	Corresponding Organ
1	1	1	1	Stomach
2	2	2	2	Lungs
3	3	3	3	Bowel
4	4	4	4	Spleen
5	5	5	5	Gall Bladder
6	6	6	6	Kidneys
7	7	7	7	Heart
8	8	8	8	Pancreas
9	9	9	9	Liver
10	10	10	10	Brain

PROBLEMS CAUSED BY MUSCULAR TENSION

Body	Chakra	Level of Perception	Function	Corresponding Organ
1	1	1	1	Stomach
2	2	2	2	Lungs
3	3	3	3	Bowel
4	4	4	4	Spleen
5	5	5	5	Gall Bladder
6	6	6	6	Kidneys
7	7	7	7	Heart
8	8	8	8	Pancreas
9	9	9	9	Liver
10	10	10	10	Brain

PROBLEMS CAUSED BY NERVOUS EXHAUSTION

Body	Chakra	Level of Understanding	Function	Corresponding Organ
1	1	1	1	Stomach
2	2	2	2	Lungs
3	3	3	3	Bowel
4	4	4	4	Spleen
5	5	5	5	Gall Bladder
6	6	6	6	Kidneys
7	7	7	7	Heart
8	8	8	8	Pancreas
9	9	9	9	Liver
10	10	10	10	Brain

PROBLEMS CAUSED BY POOR PROTECTION

Body	Chakra	Redundant Level of Knowledge	Function	Corresponding Organ
1	1	1	1	Stomach
2	2	2	2	Lungs
3	3	3	3	Bowel
4	4	4	4	Spleen
5	5	5	5	Gall Bladder
6	6	6	6	Kidneys
7	7	7	7	Heart
8	8	8	8	Pancreas
9	9	9	9	Liver
10	10	10	10	Brain

PROBLEMS CAUSED BY BLOCKED BODIES

Body	Redundant Body	Function	Corresponding Organ
1	1	1	Stomach
2	2	2	Lungs
3	3	3	Bowel
4	4	4	Spleen
5	5	5	Gall Bladder
6	6	6	Kidneys
7	7	7	Heart
8	8	8	Pancreas
9	9	9	Liver
10	10	10	Brain

PROBLEMS CAUSED BY BLOCKED LEVELS OF CONSCIOUSNESS

Body	Redundant Level of Consciousness	Level of Perception	Function	Corresponding Organ
1	1	1	1	Stomach
2	2	2	2	Lungs
3	3	3	3	Bowel
4	4	4	4	Spleen
5	5	5	5	Gall Bladder
6	6	6	6	Kidneys
7	7	7	7	Heart
8	8	8	8	Pancreas
9	9	9	9	Liver
10	10	10	10	Brain

PROBLEMS CAUSED BY BLOCKED LEVELS OF KNOWLEDGE

Body	Chakra	Redundant Level of Knowledge	Under-standing	Function	Corresponding Organ
1	1	1	1	1	Stomach
2	2	2	2	2	Lungs
3	3	3	3	3	Bowel
4	4	4	4	4	Spleen
5	5	5	5	5	Gall Bladder
6	6	6	6	6	Kidneys
7	7	7	7	7	Heart
8	8	8	8	8	Pancreas
9	9	9	9	9	Liver
10	10	10	10	10	Brain

PROBLEMS CAUSED BY BLOCKED LEVELS OF UNDERSTANDING

Body	Chakra	Redundant Level of Understanding	Function	Corresponding Organ
1	1	1	1	Stomach
2	2	2	2	Lungs
3	3	3	3	Bowel
4	4	4	4	Spleen
5	5	5	5	Gall Bladder
6	6	6	6	Kidneys
7	7	7	7	Heart
8	8	8	8	Pancreas
9	9	9	9	Liver
10	10	10	10	Brain

PROBLEMS CAUSED BY BLOCKED LEVELS OF PERCEPTION

Body	Chakra	Redundant Level of Perception	Function	Corresponding Organ
1	1	1	1	Stomach
2	2	2	2	Lungs
3	3	3	3	Bowel
4	4	4	4	Spleen
5	5	5	5	Gall Bladder
6	6	6	6	Kidneys
7	7	7	7	Heart
8	8	8	8	Pancreas
9	9	9	9	Liver
10	10	10	10	Brain

PROBLEMS CAUSED BY BLOCKED FUNCTIONS

Body	Chakra	Redundant Function	Function	Corresponding Organ
1	1	1	1	Stomach
2	2	2	2	Lungs
3	3	3	3	Bowel
4	4	4	4	Spleen
5	5	5	5	Gall Bladder
6	6	6	6	Kidneys
7	7	7	7	Heart
8	8	8	8	Pancreas
9	9	9	9	Liver
10	10	10	10	Brain

PROBLEMS CAUSED BY REDUNDANT CHAKRAS

Body	Redundant Chakra	Level of Perception	Function	Corresponding Organ
1	1	1	1	Stomach
2	2	2	2	Lungs
3	3	3	3	Bowel
4	4	4	4	Spleen
5	5	5	5	Gall Bladder
6	6	6	6	Kidneys
7	7	7	7	Heart
8	8	8	8	Pancreas
9	9	9	9	Liver
10	10	10	10	Brain

PROBLEMS CAUSED BY REDUNDANT SYSTEMS

Body	Level of Consciousness	Redundant System	Function	Corresponding Glands
1	1	1	1	Parathyroids
2	2	2	2	Pineal
3	3	3	3	Adenoids
4	4	4	4	Adrenal
5	5	5	5	Ovaries, Testes
6	6	6	6	Tonsils
7	7	7	7	Thymus
8	8	8	8	Thyroid
9	9	9	9	Pituitary
10	10	10	10	Hypothalamus

PROBLEMS CAUSED BY REDUNDANT BODIES

Body	Redundant Body	Level of Consciousness	Function	Corresponding Organ
1	1	1	1	Stomach
2	2	2	2	Lungs
3	3	3	3	Bowel
4	4	4	4	Spleen
5	5	5	5	Gall Bladder
6	6	6	6	Kidneys
7	7	7	7	Heart
8	8	8	8	Pancreas
9	9	9	9	Liver
10	10	10	10	Brain

HEALING THE SELF BY FINDING THE RIGHT PATHS
BETWEEN THE BODIES

Body	Body	Level of Consciousness	Function	Corresponding Organ
1	1	1	1	Stomach
2	2	2	2	Lungs
3	3	3	3	Bowel
4	4	4	4	Spleen
5	5	5	5	Gall Bladder
6	6	6	6	Kidneys
7	7	7	7	Heart
8	8	8	8	Pancreas
9	9	9	9	Liver
10	10	10	10	Brain

Index of Work Sheets

The British Society of Dowsers

The Society was formed in 1933 to spread information among members and the public at large on dowsing of all kinds and to keep a register of practising dowsers. The following are typical applications of the dowsing faculty.

Water location
Geophysical and site surveying
Mineral prospecting
Medical diagnosis and healing
Archaeological searches
Agricultural and soil testing

The Society has over 1000 members in this and 33 countries worldwide. People in all walks of life are members, many highly qualified in their own professions. Some are professional dowsers in their own special field and others simply those people who are interested in the art. There are a number of local groups throughout the country.

Rods, pendulums and other dowsing aids, and information are available from the Society whose Secretary and Treasurer is M.D. Rust, Esq., MBIM, of Sycamore Cottage, Tamley Lane, Hastingleigh, Ashford, Kent TN25 5HW.